CONTEMPORARY COUNTRY

EMILY CHALMERS WITH WORDS BY ALI HANAN

RYLAND
PETERS
& SMALL

LONDON NEW YORK

PHOTOGRAPHY BY DEBI TRELOAR

First published in the US in 2006 by

Ryland Peters & Small
519 Broadway, 5th Floor
New York, NY 10012
www.rylandpeters.com

10 9 8 7 6 5 4 3 2 1

Printed and bound in China.

Library of Congress Cataloging-in-Publication Data

Chalmers, Emily.
  Contemporary country / Emily Chalmers ; with words by Ali Hanan ;
photography by Debi Treloar.
     p. cm.
  Includes bibliographical references and index.
  ISBN-13: 978-1-84597-250-9 (alk. paper)
  ISBN-10: 1-84597-250-3 (alk. paper)
  1. Decoration and ornament, Rustic. 2. Interior decoration--History--
21st century. I. Hanan, Ali. II. Treloar, Debi. III. Title.
  NK1994.R87C45 2006
  747--dc22
                                        2006018038

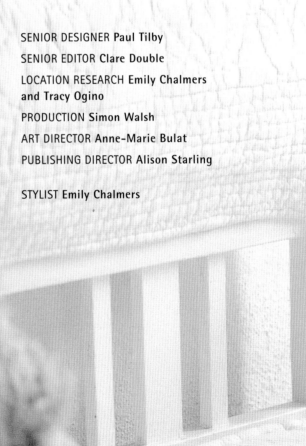

SENIOR DESIGNER Paul Tilby

SENIOR EDITOR Clare Double

LOCATION RESEARCH Emily Chalmers
and Tracy Ogino

PRODUCTION Simon Walsh

ART DIRECTOR Anne-Marie Bulat

PUBLISHING DIRECTOR Alison Starling

STYLIST Emily Chalmers

contents

introduction

There's something about contemporary country that feels just right. It takes the best of modern style, including minimalism and pared-back lines, and mixes it with down-to-earth country looks. By blending and clashing the two, you'll create an airy home that's practical, functional, and incredibly chic. A recent survey revealed that many of us now spend 90% of our lives indoors, but even within four walls we can connect to nature's roots. Our feet crave the down-to-earth feel of natural materials, like the warmth of honey-colored wood or the coolness of sandstone, while our fingertips revel in the soft touch of fluffy sheepskin, smooth linen, and cotton flannel. In a contemporary country interior, you'll feel at home with life's simple pleasures, like fresh air's changing scents, sunshine's golden light, and open-feeling interior spaces. Yet the style also embraces features of modern living, like new technologies, chic designer buys, and high-street favorites. Contemporary country is varied and eclectic, underpinned by solid, hard-working natural materials. It doesn't matter what sort of home you live in. You can bring nature-inspired artefacts into minimalist interiors, or inject urban hard-edged style into rural cottages. The mix creates a look that's easy to live with and love. This book guides you through all the elements that make up the style—atmosphere, furniture, lighting, textiles and textures, flooring, and color—and then shows you how to capture it in every room. With contemporary country, you, too, can revel in the beauty of the outdoors in your own home.

elements

In our increasingly urbanized world, nature seems an afterthought, like a solitary flower poking its head through a crack in the pavement. At the end of a long day, our inner selves yearn for a connection with nature. Nature lifts our spirits and grounds us. While contemporary country is about a style, it's also about creating a country atmosphere, even in a loft in the heart of the city.

atmosphere

One of the things we love about the country is its feeling of space and light. We love the thought that we can throw our arms open and be at one with nature itself. And that's exactly the mood you need to recreate.

First, tackle your architecture and maximize the room you've got. How can you make it more open, more spacious? Before you do anything, camp in each room in your home for a few days. Observe how the sun moves around the house and where the views and the breeze come from. Then harness it any way you can. Flesh out the space by knocking through walls, or create Arabic-style archways between rooms. Opt for floor-to-ceiling windows or extend the windows you've got. You could also consider

OPPOSITE **Bring the beauty of the outdoors inside. In a frame, you could create a piece of organic art, like this nature-inspired mood board in a kitchen, composed of fabric swatches, buttons, postcards, shell necklaces, and nature's other ornaments.**

BELOW **You could also source one kind of natural** *objet d'art,* **as this owner has done with wooden Indian printing blocks. Put eye-catching things in unexpected places to create visual surprises, like this pair of antlers mounted on a kitchen wall** (ABOVE).

taking out your back wall and installing glass folding doors to your garden to bring the outdoors in. For dark spaces, create skylights or portholes to bring in light.

Once inside, capture the light. Bright, pale, polished surfaces like stainless steel, glass, and glossy paint reflect light around rooms. Mirrors are powerful light enhancers and when placed opposite large windows can fashion new internal horizons. "Windows" cut into walls between rooms also create new vistas and provide display space.

Another way to bring in nature is to, well, literally bring it indoors. Start with flowers, one of nature's most coveted

accessories. The entrance is one area where it's essential to put an outsized bunch of flowers so whenever you walk in the door, you'll be greeted by outstretched floral arms. Have flowers beside your bed so they are the first and last things you

see. Make them unusual, as our eyes just skim over conventional posies. Create eye-catching, nose-pleasuring bunches of flowers, perhaps a huge bouquet of aromatic tiger lilies or fragrant tuberoses. Alternatively, scatter rose petals on the ledge around your bathtub or place flowers in teacups along windowsills: make unexpected natural "arrangements" where they would be least expected.

One way of making nature a feature is to include larger-than-life indoor plants, such as a pair of giant cacti (see picture on page 51), leafy palm trees, or spiky yuccas. Almost like living sculptures, these plants also help to purify the air.

While bringing in living nature adds a natural *joie de vivre* to your interiors, other natural motifs and objects inject country life. Floral motifs on cushions, teacups, lampshades, and almost anywhere else bring in a country feel. Display other *objets trouvés* from beach walks and

In this potter's house, a sense of country springs from a mix of natural, traditional, and contemporary pieces, arranged to make the most of light and space. In the bedroom (ABOVE LEFT), a wicker chair and table sit beneath a window, while in the living room downstairs, a quilted daybed makes a sunny spot to revel in a garden view (ABOVE RIGHT). The floral theme is repeated throughout: in the kitchen, (OPPOSITE), flowers adorn dainty teacups, wall tiles, and dishtowels. The studio is crowned by a lampshade fashioned from an old bowl (OPPOSITE BELOW LEFT), while old vases and bowls house odds and ends in a work room (LEFT).

Leave your home's rustic charm exposed, as seen in this house's cracked plaster walls, peeling paint, ancient weathered woods, and sturdy iron door latches. Many old fixtures, like door handles and window latches, were built to last, so reinstate salvaged examples where you can, or revive existing ones. Choose handmade things, like hand-painted bowls, hand-thrown pots, and children's artworks, as they possess a human spirit, unlike the too-polished looks of machine-made pieces. The curtains, by famed wool craftsman Kaffe Fassett, blend natural colors in undulating rhythms and provide a soft, insulating cover for the windows. To counter the home's rough feel, the owner has draped an armchair with a pure white cotton cover and a table in soft-weave linens.

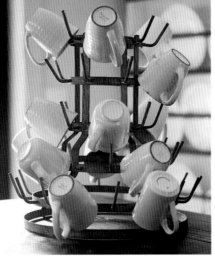

Don't hide your collections away. In big country kitchens, dishes were often displayed on plate racks (FAR LEFT) or on shelves. Here this owner has gone one step farther and created a mug tree from an old bottle storage unit (LEFT).

While your vases wait for flowers, you could show off your collection (BELOW).

Display your collections of things like china plates, antique teacups, copper cooking pots, hand-thrown vases, or whatever takes your fancy.

forest strolls, like pine cones, driftwood, colored stones and pebbles, shells, and more. They'll remind you of the moment you found them.

Small details also reveal who we are and what we love. They tell stories of the past and provoke memories, and even add interior wit. So display your collections of things like china plates, antique teacups, copper cooking pots, hand-thrown vases, or whatever takes your fancy.

Nature can also be immortalized. If you have time, make leaves into prints or press flowers in books. For an impromptu piece of natural art, simply buy an old frame and a piece of canvas and make an artwork of pressed and dried flowers. Otherwise, you could hang up bunches of dried flowers or dry pumpkins and gourds and put them on display. You can also seek out nature-inspired artefacts with a slightly kitsch twist, like pinned butterflies in frames, cabbage-leaf plates, ceramic flying ducks for the wall, clay pigeons, or fake flowers.

While visual stimuli play the most important role in creating an atmosphere, don't forget your other senses. Just the slightest whiff of natural scents can put us at ease. Lavender's scent is said to be relaxing, so harvest lavender from your garden, dry it, and sew it into linen pouches to put beneath your pillow. Essential oils distill some of nature's purest scents into a bottle. You can bring in a wide range of scents—rosemary, mint, sandalwood, lavender, geranium—let your nose guide you. Just add a few drops to water in a burner and light a votive candle underneath.

Fresh air brings its own aromas, so open windows whenever you can and allow life-giving oxygen to waft and weave through your house. Even

In the kitchen (RIGHT), this owner has fashioned a sense of country from antique pieces such as large creamware plates, vintage carafes, antique silver toast racks, and collections of thick country china. These old pieces are contrasted with wall-mounted shelves, which give a twist of modernity. While the cooktop is modern, the bench top also has an old butler's sink, a vintage wall-mounted soap dish, and original brass faucets.

THIS PAGE With its bright white walls and airy feeling of space, this dining room possesses a sense of the outdoors. A large bowl of country objects, including a deer's antlers, creates a sculptural centerpiece for the room. To give the color scheme depth, the wood table is black and the walls pure white. For an informal look, the high-backed chairs are swathed in loose-fitting ticking covers.

OPPOSITE White on white is a contemporary classic, particularly for rooms that demand peace and quiet, like bedrooms and bathrooms. Yet this combination can be stark—it has been warmed up here with white's gentler tones like soft creams and magnolia. For indoor flower displays, try amaryllis—they last a long time and can be grown from bulbs.

urban smells like the rain on warm pavements or a whiff of damp leaves tells us of the seasons and keeps us in touch with nature's rhythms. Potted plants are natural air filters, absorbing toxins and oxygenating the air. Superhero air-conditioners are gerbera daisies, Boston ferns, bamboo palms, English ivy, spider plants, and weeping figs.

One of the other sensual qualities of the country we treasure is its peace and quiet; to stand in a field and hear nothing except the sounds of the birds going about their business. This aural tranquility is hard to find in the city, but have floors soundproofed and install triple-glazing if you can.

Water, with its soothing, calming negative ions, removes the positive ions created by electricity from the air, which is why a walk on the beach or a post-thunderstorm deluge feels so refreshing. For many people, the sound of running water is a tonic for jangled nerves, so if possible, create an indoor fountain. Otherwise, buy a couple of goldfish and enjoy the peaceful sight of fish swimming around.

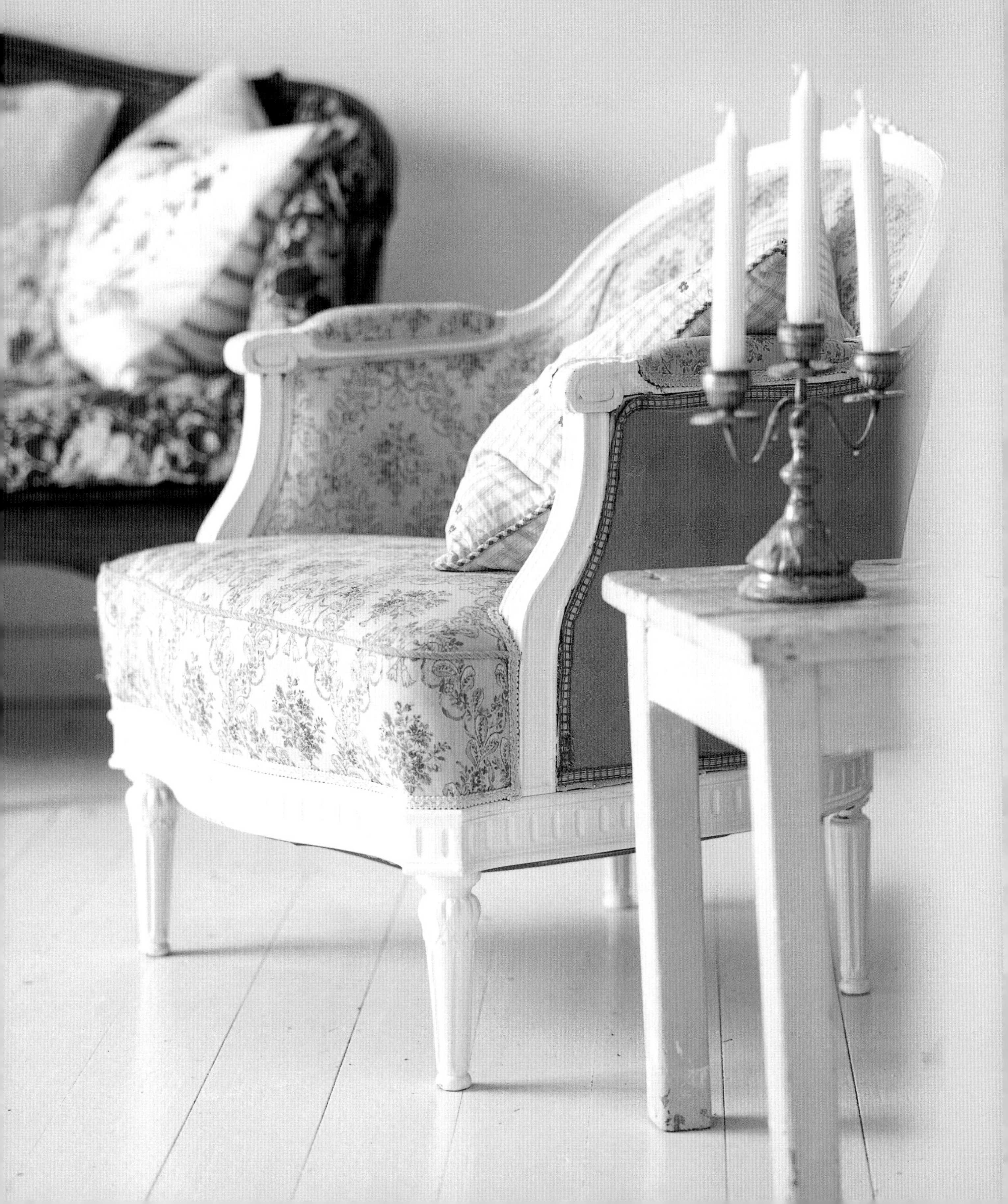

furnishings

LEFT Give beautiful pieces of furniture center stage by keeping a room's canvases, the floors and walls, in plain colors and textures. For a relaxed country look, cover seating with a quilt, bedspread, or throw.

ABOVE LEFT **Exquisite pieces, like the two-seater above, can double as** *objets d'art.*

ABOVE RIGHT **For graceful dining, choose a Gustavian-style table and chairs and take the Scandinavian feel further by painting walls and floors off-white.**

Contemporary country furnishings are an eclectic bunch. Take the range of chairs, for example, which spans from modern bentwood Scandinavian designs sourced from the mall to traditional high-backed dining chairs unearthed in antique stores. What you choose will depend on your interior, but they will all have something in common. They'll be crafted from natural materials.

Plastic furniture became fashionable in the Fifties. Even teacups were made from melamine, and sofas were coated with vinyl. Furniture became disposable. However, manmade furniture's qualities pale beside natural pieces. Plastics are easily scarred by daily wear and tear. Once used or broken, plastic furniture is only fit for the scrapheap—hardly environmentally friendly. If you do buy plastic furniture, opt for retro pieces from the Fifties and Sixties, with organic shapes. They are made from more robust plastics and, of course, have proven longevity.

Furniture created from natural materials is easily rejuvenated. There are craftsmen dedicated to reweaving wicker furniture and reupholstering antique chairs. Even modern classics are easily restored. Wooden slats are replaceable, a chipped chair is quickly repainted, and threadbare arms can be given a patch or disguised under a beautiful blanket. When these pieces do come to the end of their natural lives, they can sometimes be turned into other objects. The reasons to invest in nature's beautiful pieces are endless.

When selecting furniture, think of where a piece will live. If your backdrops are neutral, choose items with interesting

THIS PAGE **For a sedate feel in keeping with the contemporary country look, choose Shaker-style furniture with strong, simple lines. The antique settle below has been reupholstered with a stylish cotton squab. Unless you're going to make a feature of your heating, keep it discreet, as seen with this baseboard heater.**

OPPOSITE **Choose a daybed with a light muslin cover** (FOREGROUND) **or a large high-backed sofa big enough for two to sink into** (BACKGROUND) **for relaxing at the end of a long day.**

shapes or those upholstered in lively patterned fabrics. With busy patterned backdrops, go for pieces that won't create visual overload, like a quiet nut-brown leather sofa or a plain wicker chair in a simple shape. Contrast pieces with their setting, too—if your interior is ultra-modern, give it a sense of history with some beautiful antique furniture. If you have a rag-rolled, crackled wall, put a contemporary piece in front of it. Creating visual juxtapositions with furniture sparks a room into life.

Seating is one of the main purchases you'll make. From curvaceous modern seats to

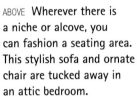

ABOVE Wherever there is
a niche or alcove, you
can fashion a seating area.
This stylish sofa and ornate
chair are tucked away in
an attic bedroom.

LEFT Mix and match old
country pieces, like this
rustic wooden table, with
contemporary pieces, such
as this modern classic sofa
and chair.

high-backed formal chairs, a huge variety will suit the look.
However, choose chairs with natural coverings as they will
fit best with your décor. Before you buy, consider the shape
and proportions of the room. If you have low ceilings, for
example, low-level seating will preserve a sense of space.
Chairs crafted from wood have always been contemporary
country's favorite. Wood is smooth and warm to touch.
It's the material favored by Scandinavian designers such
as Arne Jacobsen, Hans Wegner, and Alvar Aalto. If you
don't like traditional furniture, these designers and British
counterparts like Tom Dixon and Matthew Hilton have
created contemporary classics. Wicker chairs are also
comforting to sit on. Lloyd Loom chairs, with their curved
backs and generous seats, are worth the investment.

OPPOSITE BELOW Clothed in a warm, rich leather, this chrome chair looks very modern, yet a tiled floor, a stack of sawn logs, and a dyed sheepskin all work together to give the overall look a rustic spin.

THIS PAGE A curvy, modern basketweave chair and retro Sixties' sideboard contrast with this room's more traditional elements such as the original planks on the floor, the wooden side table, and the gilt-framed picture. To soften the look and add depth to the color scheme, the owner has added a large black-and-white cowhide.

THIS PAGE The subtle grain of white leather on this comfortable dining chair contrasts with the smooth lines of a modern wooden table. In the background, a huge laundry basket is home to a pile of logs. The owner has chosen simple furniture to complement the sophisticated patina of the parquet-style tongue-and-groove wall. If your backdrop is patterned, choose plain pieces, and vice versa, to create visual harmony.

OPPOSITE LEFT Bar stools perch at a breakfast bar in this contemporary country kitchen. For a seamless look, floor-to-ceiling storage has been built in, dispensing with the need for freestanding furniture.

OPPOSITE RIGHT Instead of a predictable set of dining chairs, collect an assortment of a similar height and material. Then, as this owner has done, add ticking squabs to the seats to unite them. The dining table is simply an enormous plank on trestles.

If you can't find the right number of chairs, hand-pick an assortment with a similar look, such as wire-framed chairs or wooden chairs with high backs.

The main criteria for choosing a chair must be function and ease. As always, try any chair before you buy. A chair that isn't comfortable after five minutes certainly won't be any better after you've been sitting in it for a couple of hours. However, don't forget you can soften a chair's hard edges with squabs, cushions, and rugs.

For an original look, source secondhand chairs and give them your own twist. Take a 20th-century piece, for example, and swathe it in a country-style cover, like a vintage paisley, stripes, or florals. Conversely, take antiques like chaises longues and high-back chairs and bring them up to date with modern upholstery or adorn them with cushions covered in funky fabrics.

You can create your own furniture by heading down to a reclamation yard and salvaging old bits of lumber. Cut up thick trunks, sand and varnish them, and turn them into stools; reclaim old railroad ties, sand them,

varnish them, and pile them up against the wall, where they will become useful bench seats.

One piece of furniture that seems to transcend time is the leather sofa. Leather is incredibly hard-wearing, as antique leather furniture testifies. If the leather is past its sell-by date, but its springs, stuffing, and frame are sturdy, you can have a sofa reupholstered. If you keep leather supple, moist, and well nourished, it will endure, so use a proprietary cream to prevent it from drying and cracking.

When buying a sofa, choose a generously large one with soft, yet supportive cushions. Again, if you like a sofa's shape, you can always reupholster it—for a country look, you could choose red-and-white striped canvas, vintage florals, or plain blocks of color with an assortment of multicolored cushions.

If you don't like sitting shoulder to shoulder with others, opt for armchairs, chaises longues, or daybeds. Other chairs

from offbeat sources, like old church pews, school chairs, office chairs, and antique dental chairs, can also have the right look. You may like to put your feet up and recline in contemporary country style. Bring a wicker sunlounger indoors and deck it with cushions, or simply find a single bed, push it up against the wall, and create an impromptu daybed by scattering it with pillows.

In the kitchen, one of contemporary country's mainstays is an enormous farmhouse table, generously wide, long,

and sturdy. These old tables are now hard to find, but other antique tables also suit the look, such as former leather-cutting tables, old boardroom tables, or long, thin French vineyard tables, originally used for sorting grapes. Otherwise, pick anything of a suitable size, from an office desk to a school desk, and give it a modern makeover with paint or hide it under a big tablecloth.

For modern tables, choose a wooden one with simple lines or create your own from a smooth door mounted on trestles. If you're short of space, go for a flexible option such as a table with drop leaves. A more offbeat idea is to hang a door from pulleys on the ceiling and lower it whenever you need a work space or a table for a dinner party. Side tables, stacking tables, and occasional tables provide convenient surfaces on which to perch mugs, books, and lamps, and are useful as display spaces.

Again, when it comes to choosing dining chairs, aim for visual dichotomy. Put old garden chairs beside a slick glass table or contemporary chairs around an antique farmhouse version. If you can't find the right number of chairs for your table, go eclectic and hand-pick an assortment of seats with a similar look, such as wire-framed chairs or wooden chairs with high backs. For a modern look, you could build a long picnic-table-style bench made from sustainable woods in a clean-lined style.

Good storage is key to the contemporary country look, since you want to preserve a sense of uncluttered space. However, homes with nothing on display seem stark and

empty, so mix various storage options, including shelves and alcoves to show off ornaments and photographs.

For small storage choices, keep to the ethos and avoid succumbing to plastic boxes. Instead, house your videos, magazines, and odds and ends in wicker baskets, metal pails, milk jugs, antique leather suitcases, wooden crates, and old shoeboxes covered in vintage papers.

For large-scale storage, choose antique armoires, tea chests, and chests of drawers, which you can always sand and repaint. If you find antique pieces with hand-painted motifs and peeling paint, leave them as they are and they'll fit in beautifully with the look. Old hutches

ABOVE LEFT **A former school desk now makes a pedestal for nature's ornaments.**

ABOVE RIGHT **Reclaim old chests of drawers. They are often sturdier than their flat-pack counterparts as they were crafted to last from thick, robust woods. Sand them and rediscover their woody good looks, or make them over with a coat of chalky white paint.**

THIS PICTURE **Many modern wooden pieces come with simple, pared-back lines, like this stylish side table.**

with shelves to display china are beautiful and useful in a contemporary country home. Display your best pieces on the shelves and tuck everyday china underneath. Sideboards, particularly wooden styles from the Fifties and Sixties, are classics and the perfect place to store living-room items. Old-fashioned pieces such as cocktail cabinets and trolleys also provide unusual-looking storage areas. Otherwise, re-fashion and employ office furniture such as filing cabinets, or create country-style storage from stacks of wooden fruit boxes. Be inventive.

If you're living in a modern home, you can always build in your storage. You can hide your clutter completely by creating a built-in wall of storage using wooden panels with push catches, or build cupboards under the stairs.

Small details count, so finding the right fixtures is important. If you've chosen a modern bathtub, for example, you could add Victorian faucets. Door handles are equally important—they are a home's handshake—so choose antique doorknobs or metal latch fixtures. If you'd rather not distract the eye from the beauty of old wooden doors, add delicate glass doorknobs that look barely there.

This leggy desk looks elegant next to the high-backed sofa. Beside the natural canvas of the sofa, the owner has put a cluster of details including pebbles, a white ceramic dish, a metal pitcher, and a glass bottle. The red berries inject vitality and vibrancy to a room of cool neutrals. Without them, the room might feel lifeless.

Make the most of your home's natural good looks. Expose old wooden beams, strip floors to reveal old brickwork, and leave stone fireplaces untouched, as seen here. These features give a home a sense of history. Install reclaimed pieces like this old wooden door, which has been given a minimalist twist with a trio of cut-out windows to let through light and air.

When converting this barn, the owners preserved and exposed the original beams, leaving the architecture to tell the building's story. This is a children's bedroom in the eaves. To complement the nut-brown color of the beams, the ceiling is a tongue-and-groove pattern, painted fresh lime white.

The textiles and textures of natural materials are all honest and hard-working. They are more robust than their manmade counterparts, and in some ways they seem as if they were tailor-made for use in the home.

textures & textiles

Take wool, for example, which can bend up to thirty thousand times without breaking. Perfect, then, to weave into rugs to soften your steps. Or linen, which is three times stronger when wet: ideal for dishtowels. For floors, nature brings us wood and stone. We can tread on them endlessly and they just seem to get better with wear. Wood begins to feel softer, while stone just gets tiny shiny patches even after it has been trodden on by countless feet. Nature seems to have created materials just for our interiors.

Floors, walls, and ceilings are backdrops to your beautiful things, so keep their textures simple and neutral. For more about floors, see Underfoot (pages 42–47). When adorning the walls, think of them as your home's skin. Your furniture,

paintings, ornaments, and plants will bring in their own color, so keep this backdrop neutral. However, country style—like nature—is never perfect, so leave any natural blemishes and highlight any natural beauty spots like weathered timbers, old tiles, and brickwork, or leave in place patches of antique wallpaper.

If you live in a modern building, cover your walls with natural materials. A Scandinavian favorite is tongue-and-groove wood paneling, which you can paint white or leave in its natural honeyed tones. Another contemporary twist uses all the different tones of wood to create a smooth, subtle backdrop. Buy different-colored wooden panels and put them side by side. For a decadent touch, try leather tiles on your walls. Wallpapers now come in a vast array of designs—and those include a huge range of natural motifs. Wallpapering a whole room may be too much on the eye, so for a contemporary look, paper just one wall and coat the rest in a soft, chalky paint.

Choose textural finishes that give a home a warm, inviting personality. Just as a too-perfect friend is difficult to live with, you will find a too-perfect home impossible to live

ABOVE **Take a leaf out of an interior stylist's book and use your own clothing and accessories, like this modern scarf and designer leather handbag, to provide contrasts.**

LEFT **Juxtapose sophisticated fabrics with country materials, as in this textural trio of fluffy sheepskin, smooth caramel leather, and glamorous sequins.**

OPPOSITE ABOVE LEFT **A Norfolk latch looks stunning after decades of use.**

OPPOSITE ABOVE RIGHT **A smooth white modern wall seems even more stylish opposite raw whitewashed wood.**

OPPOSITE BELOW LEFT **Huge hewn logs create a dramatic entrance way and promise a warm, cozy interior.**

OPPOSITE BELOW CENTER **Soften raw edges with a feminine twist of silky fabrics, like this Indian bedspread and satin cushions.**

OPPOSITE BELOW RIGHT **Pile wool hand-knits and blankets together to allay any hard edges.**

One way to soften country's raw, naked looks is to cover windows with natural fabrics.

CLOCKWISE FROM ABOVE This window cover has been sewn out of old embroidered tablecloths; for a soft look, add ties to a cotton sheet and fasten the curtain to an antique wrought-iron pole with big bows; a swathe of muslin with a burlap edge lets through light, but not prying eyes; lace on the back of a door or over a window highlights its delicate pattern, but also lets in light and air.

OPPOSITE Country is about rough, ready looks, like this cupboard coated with distressed paintwork, while contemporary is about smooth modern lines, such as the angular window frame, curvy dining chairs, and polished tabletop.

in or maintain. Besides, a home's character lines are in its time-worn details, like weathered floorboards, slightly peeling paint on walls, and shiny patches on bricks from endless footsteps.

In this pared-back yet simple setting, solid textures—wood, metal, stone, and glass—can seem too hard and stark. That's where fabrics come in. Soft furnishings mellow the look, allay hard edges, and give a natural interior a country twist. When you put textural surfaces, like walls and pieces of furniture, together with textiles, you'll find that by contrasting them, you'll emphasize their looks. Juxtapose rough textures with smooth, sophisticated textiles. Drape delicate white lace tablecloths over your old

> As it's thin, silk makes a perfect summer covering for windows. Voile is another one, letting light diffuse softly through its loose weaves.

wooden farmhouse table, for example, or coarse hemp curtains over your smooth contemporary windows. You could also use embroidered linen tablecloths, initialed handkerchiefs, and other hand-worked textiles. If bought secondhand, re-interpret them for modern life.

Natural fabrics are far superior to their manmade counterparts. They let through light, air, and aromas. You only need to sweat in a polyester shirt on a hot day and compare it to wearing a cotton one to appreciate the difference. The same applies to covers for chairs or anywhere fabrics come into contact with the skin.

Natural fibers such as wool, linen, and cotton have incredible properties. Wool is a great insulator. Wool from Romney sheep is suitable for carpets, while Merino wool, a soft, high-luster yarn, is spun into the finest plaid blankets and throws. Wool forms many traditional fabrics, such as tartan plaids and tweeds, that blend seamlessly into a country-style home.

Linen, made from the flax plant, was once worth its weight in gold. With the rise of cheaper cottons, it lost its allure, but now stashes of antique linens are surfacing at markets and specialty shops. You might find a bargain, but linen sheets are an investment; sleeping between them is one of life's luxuries.

Cotton is one of the oldest fabrics in the world. Cheaper and easier to produce than

OPPOSITE **Treat a room's floor, ceilings, and walls as canvases on which to create eye-catching surfaces, like this tongue-and-groove ceiling and tile floor.**

ABOVE LEFT **Mix country patterns, like florals and paisleys, with plains, such as ticking fabrics, as seen on this wooden daybed.**

ABOVE RIGHT **A rattan sofa is dressed with a comforter and an array of scatter cushions in cotton florals and stripes.**

LEFT **When you're next at a flea market or fabric outlet, buy bolts of ticking fabric and sew cushion covers for summer garden chairs.**

Reclaim fabrics from farmhouse sources, like antique flour sacks and grain sacks, and use them and mattress ticking to make original cushions.

linen, cotton is made in a huge range of thicknesses, styles, and patterns. Cotton ticking, in red and white stripes, is a country favorite, as are traditional florals and ginghams. Other cottons synonymous with hard-working country style are chambray, originally from Chambrai in France, and denim (from Nîmes), which both look at home in country-style soft furnishings.

Silk, with its soft, natural luster, adds a sense of luxury to any home and yet is incredibly hard-wearing. As it's thin, silk makes a perfect summer covering for windows. Humble cotton voile has been reinstated as a coveted fabric. Again, it's a perfect summer window covering,

letting light diffuse softly through its loose weaves. Other natural fabrics at home in a contemporary country setting are the rough weaves of horsehair, hemp, and burlap. Canvas makes a thick, practical cover suitable for sofas and armchairs.

Animal skins once clothed us and gave us warmth, so there is something primal about covering a floor in a large brown-and-white cowhide or placing a baby on a soft sheepskin. Animal skins provide warmth and visual softness. Adorn your sofas with secondhand finds like rabbit skins, or cover your floors with thicker, more robust alternatives such as cowhide or goatskin.

OPPOSITE LEFT **Instead of an artwork on the wall, create an area of visual interest with an assortment of cushions in all sizes.**

OPPOSITE RIGHT **Reclaim fabrics from farmhouse sources, like antique flour sacks and grain sacks, and use them and mattress ticking to make original scatter cushions, like these seen on a modern, four-poster daybed.**

THIS PAGE **This statement headboard for a contemporary bedroom is made out of an old hand-buttoned mattress fastened to a metal pole. The large striped cushions on the bed complement the blue-and-white headboard.**

There is something special about feeling the earth beneath your feet, like the softness of freshly mown grass, the warmth of the sun on smooth stone, or the feeling of your toes sinking into fine sand. Feeling connected with the earth literally grounds us. Feet have thousands of receptive nerve endings, so do your soles a favor and cover your floors with a natural material.

underfoot

Natural floorings feel like they're part of a real, solid home. Certain natural flooring options, like flagstones and some hardwoods, are certainly a big investment. However, although they are expensive, they age with grace and will last longer than you. Before making a purchase, consider your needs. For example, if you have small children, you'll want something easy to clean—wool carpets are kind to tiny knees, but prone to stains, so tuck them away in adult-only areas like a master bedroom or bathroom. Thick-

OPPOSITE Flagstone floors in this old farmhouse retain their good looks after years of use. Stone is one of nature's most enduring floor coverings, but without underfloor heating it can feel cold.

ABOVE LEFT Think of an outdoor patio indoors and create a textural floor from patterned brickwork. To offset its warm terra cotta hues and provide a visual divide between the floor and walls, the baseboards are painted black.

ABOVE RIGHT This sweeping staircase becomes a feature with its striking black-and-white color scheme. Glossy floors keep the overall look light and spacious.

> **Look for wood from sustainable forests, like oak, elm, pine, spruce, and walnut. For a modern look, opt for extra-wide floorboards.**

weave jute matting is practical and hard-wearing, but it's rough and will be unsuitable if you like walking with bare feet on your living-room floor or you have a baby. Also, like carpet, this kind of surface is prone to stains. Areas with a lot of household traffic, such as entrances, stairs, and kitchens, need a sturdy, easy-to-clean flooring such as tiles, wood, or flagstones. Cleanable rugs can help define areas, for example, a dining area in a kitchen.

Wooden floors were one of the trends of the Nineties, yet really they have been in vogue for centuries. If you're lucky, you may find a wooden floor beneath old carpet awaiting stripping, sanding, and restoring; if not, buy a quality floor of sustainable wood. Old wood is often thicker, richer in patina, and better in quality than new. Find boards at architectural salvage yards, which are also a source of tropical hardwoods like mahogany, ebony, teak, rosewood, and wenge. These are all endangered woods, and most are thankfully now protected. If you're buying new boards, look for wood from sustainable "second-growth" forests, like oak, elm, pine, spruce, and walnut. For a modern look, opt for extra-wide floorboards; for a traditional look, consider laying a parquet floor.

Once your boards are laid, give them a good sanding, then varnish them or wax with beeswax for its aromatic, antistatic finish. If you like the Scandinavian white-on-white look, apply a soft wash of diluted organic latex, then seal with shellac, a natural varnish. Alternatives to wood, which come with the warm, woody hues but not the price tag, include cork (made by stripping the bark of the cork oak) and linoleum (made from powdered cork, linseed oil, wood flour, chalk, and wood resins).

ABOVE LEFT **This wooden floor has a high-gloss varnish, which reflects the light and keeps the interior feeling airy and open.**

ABOVE CENTER AND LEFT **If you can, strip floor coverings and see if there are wooden boards underneath. These homeowners were lucky. Otherwise, if you have an old wooden floor that's looking a bit worn, sand it, stain it, and coat it with natural varnish to increase its life expectancy. If you don't have an old floor, but prefer the look of old wood, buy wooden boards from architectural salvage yards.**

OPPOSITE **For a clean, contemporary look, choose wide floorboards.**

OPPOSITE ABOVE **This floor has been fashioned from polished concrete, which could look austere in an empty space but comes to life when teamed with the wooden table, antique candlesticks, and a garden view. Concrete flooring can be cold underfoot— perfect for long, hot summers. For happy feet in the winter months, underfloor heating is a great advantage.**

OPPOSITE BELOW LEFT **Think of how an area will be used before you choose flooring. Polished concrete is a solid, easy-to-clean choice for an entrance way.**

OPPOSITE BELOW RIGHT **Polished rubber makes a durable floor that's quick to clean— and it's perfect for children.**

THIS PAGE **Concrete steps, covered with a milky whitewash, give this flight of stairs a monastic look.**

Stone comes with a heavy price tag, but almost no other material will serve you so well. It lasts a lifetime and beyond, as the smooth, slightly shiny patches on the steps of centuries-old buildings testify. Stone comes in a number of colors, from the deep, dark gray of Welsh slate to the soft, chalky white of limestone. Check with an expert before you lay your stone, as some varieties are porous and may need sealing to prevent staining.

Other floor coverings include tiles and bricks, which come in earthy, warm tones from terra cotta (which means "burnt earth") to ocher yellow. Tiles can be laid in patterns or alternated with other colors to give the floor vibrancy. Natural materials like burlap, jute, and seagrass matting have also walked onto our homes' floors more and more over the last half-century. These thick grass fibers are incredibly resilient and come in a choice of neutral shades.

Last, there's oh-so-soft carpet. For the longest-lasting carpet, choose 100% pure wool. It may cost you a little more, but it will look alluring for years. Not only that but, according to the New Zealand Wool Board, wool can purify and cleanse the air by absorbing contaminants like formaldehyde, nitrogen dioxide, and sulfur dioxide, which are often found in the air inside our homes.

THIS PAGE A contemporary scheme of white walls and acres of nut-brown woods needs plenty of bright accents. This owner has opted for brilliant reds, seen on the pillows, the saucer, and the floral towel. The red is calmed by the light gray-blue lampshade.

OPPOSITE LEFT Without the striking modern red lampshade, this interior would feel too sedate.

OPPOSITE RIGHT Gray-blue and white is a fresh Scandinavian-style combination, yet it needs the reds in the background for a spark of *joie de vivre*.

In our lexicon, we only have a handful of words for actual colors, like pink, yellow, red, blue, brown, black, white, purple, green, and gray. The rest of the words we use for color come from references to what we see —and so much of that derives from nature itself. If you imagine your favorite hues, what you'll probably see in your mind's eye are natural tints, like the deep blood red of a rose, the fresh green of a new leaf, or the bright blue of a summer sky.

color

Nature defines color. We talk of colors in terms of the landscape (terra cotta, peat, sandy yellow, stone, slate gray), flowers (poppy red, buttercup yellow, snowdrop white), gemstones (aquamarine, turquoise,

moonstone, amethyst), trees (walnut brown, mahogany, ebony), fruits (tangerine, cherry red, avocado), and the list goes on and on.

Consider also the physical way we see color. As Newton demonstrated, white light can be split into a spectrum of color, beginning with violet, which has a short resonant wavelength, and ending in red, which has a long, slow wavelength. In the middle sits green—and the eye barely has to work at all to look at the color green. That's why it's thought of as a "balancing" color. In a room, green and pale colors retreat; strong, warm colors advance. So, to create the illusion of space, opt for colors with heavy tints of white, or to make a room seem cozy, go for strong reds.

Color also has a quiet influence on us. For many of us this is deeply personal; many memories and associations with color are buried in our subconscious. Buried within our psyche, different colors can hold an extra

level of meaning than the visual. Green, for example, is a universal symbol of life and abundance—it's our color oasis. Blue, the world's most popular hue, is the color of the two elements that are vital for life: air and water.

Many of us are oddly shy about using colors in our interiors. In fact, the most popular paint color is cream-white magnolia. Yet living with color, particularly nature's hues, can change the way a home feels. The trick is to find the right shades. You'll have to sample a few. Buy small tester tins, paint a large patch of color on your wall, and watch how it changes in different lights. Try the colors that magnetize you and experiment with new ones. For example, many of us think blue is too cool to live with. Try, then, blue's warmer tones of lavender, mauve, indigo, and purple, and bring it to life with fresh contrasts of orange, yellow, and white. You may think you couldn't live with green, but sample some of its many shades, like pea green, apple greens, forest greens, mints, olives, moss, copper green, jade, emerald, and lime, and you may change your mind.

Nature comes with her own neutrals, such as slate, pebble, ocher, clay, oatmeal, plum, and eggplant. These hues bring us an almost primal connection with the earth. They can be earthy or elegant, subtle or dominant, rustic or modernist. The beauty of neutrals is that they are easy to live with; these colors blend in effortlessly with nature's other materials, like lace, linen, hemp, and wood. Yet neutrals need

The beauty of neutrals is that they are easy to live with; these colors blend in effortlessly with natural materials like lace, linen, hemp, and wood.

ABOVE **A white-on-white color scheme can look too austere, so bring it to life with contrasts of black and mid-tones of cream, brown, and stone. When combining colors, you can bring in a little visual drama with opposing colors and then soften them by using several tones. There are dozens of shades of white to choose from, but for a country look, choose warmer tones of cream or pearl.**

This living room's colors resemble a seashore on an overcast day: all the colors are subtle but mix effortlessly together. The tones of natural materials also form a seamless palette of neutrals.

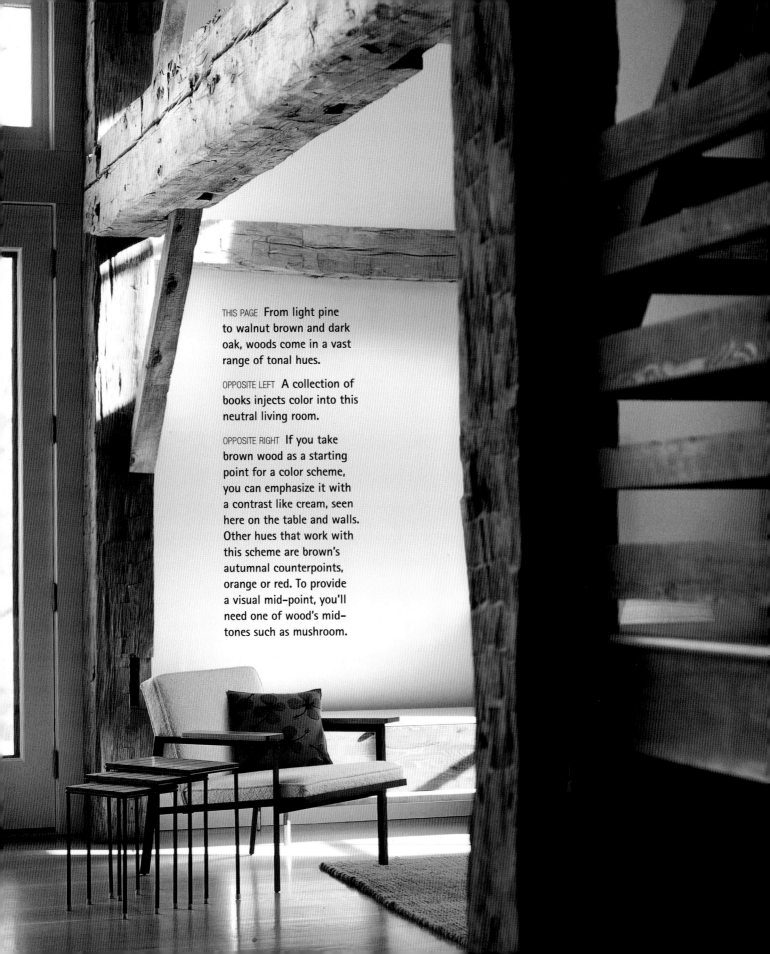

THIS PAGE **From light pine to walnut brown and dark oak, woods come in a vast range of tonal hues.**

OPPOSITE LEFT **A collection of books injects color into this neutral living room.**

OPPOSITE RIGHT **If you take brown wood as a starting point for a color scheme, you can emphasize it with a contrast like cream, seen here on the table and walls. Other hues that work with this scheme are brown's autumnal counterpoints, orange or red. To provide a visual mid-point, you'll need one of wood's mid-tones such as mushroom.**

contrasts; otherwise, an interior can feel too subdued. The colors can look monotonous. Dark browns and blacks will provide a neutral room with visual full stops, while cream, buttermilk, and fresh white will breathe in space.

Nature often has her own way of adding contrasts, however. Against her backdrops of green, brown, or blue, there is always a surprise. Even in the depths of winter, red holly berries flash against dark leaves. Her schemes are also never predictable. In the English spring, for example, you'll often see a dark gray sky contrasted with a field of fluorescent yellow rapeseed.

Before you begin your scheme, keep some of the rules of color combining in mind. Colors that sit beside each other in the spectrum, like greens and blues, are "harmonious" colors; "tones," such as sky blue and navy blue, are part of a color's extended family; and "contrasts" are colors that sit opposite each other, for example purple and yellow, or red and green. To create your own scheme, you need a mix of colors. Too many harmonious colors make an interior feel bland and lifeless, while a surfeit of

contrasts adds too much visual noise to a room. The trick is to find a balance within your palette.

When you picture most of nature's vistas, there's always a blend of color harmonies, tones, and contrasts. To decide your color scheme, imagine your most-loved natural setting. Let your imagination wander. You could take your color inspiration from the Amazon jungle, with its palm greens, mahogany browns, and flecks of riotous oranges, fiery yellows, and hot pinks, or from a field in Provence in late summer, with sunflower yellows, cobalt blues, salmon pinks, lavenders, and leafy greens.

Otherwise, you could let the seasons dictate your palette. For a spring scheme, you could go for fresh snowdrop whites, deep blues, fresh greens, and accents of pastel yellow. Summer celebrates multicolor: just think of a meadow full of wild flowers, like poppy reds, daisy whites, grassy green, and a deep sky blue. In the fall, the palette changes to burnt browns, rusty reds, deep oranges, and dark greens. Last, winter brings its cool range of grays, browns, blacks, and snow-whites.

A large hanging shade in red transforms this space. It becomes a visual focal point, taking a sedate color scheme into a realm of its own. Natural light comes in by day from a skylight above the dining table.

light

Once sunlight dictated what we did with our days. When night fell, firelight and candles allowed us to "burn the midnight oil." Now light comes in so many different forms. We can still enjoy rustic traditions of firelight, but also indulge in contemporary lighting, like halogen spotlights, twinkling fairy lights, and glamorous chandeliers.

ABOVE LEFT **A woven basket pendant light hangs low, casting a slatted glow over this comfortable living room. Low-hanging lights won't work in rooms with low ceilings as the eye is drawn down, making the ceiling seem even lower.**

ABOVE RIGHT **For a modern look, group lights in twos and threes, as seen in this simple white pendant duet. In the evening, this duo provides a swathe of bright light across the table, and the white shades diffuse a softer, more ambient light around the room.**

RIGHT **An abundance of clear, bright light is an unsung material in itself. A flood of natural light also mimics the country's feeling of space and airiness. Eschew curtains and keep window frames bare to let in as much light as possible.**

At the flick of an electric switch, home lighting turned from natural to artificial sources. Now most of us spend the majority of our time indoors under artificial light, yet exposure to sunlight helps us produce vitamin D and helps the body heal. Without it, we suffer. In winter, when sunlight is just one tenth of its summer intensity, some of us are affected by the "winter blues," suffering from SAD (Seasonal Affective Disorder). The remedy is natural light.

To keep your home and your spirit uplifted, you need to maximize the natural light that reaches you. For a start, spend a day or two watching the light move around your home, then organize your rooms around the amount of

ABOVE LEFT **Every kitchen
needs a mix of task and
ambient lighting.** Here the
warm glow from a row of
halogen spotlights mounted
on a long thin rail is a
practical way of providing
a clear, bright overall light.

ABOVE CENTER **Stylish bell-
shaped ceramic light shades
add an elegant note to
country's rough looks.**

LEFT **A trio of sculptural
white shades in a mix of
shapes act as a modern
counterpoint to this home's
rustic architecture.**

OPPOSITE ABOVE RIGHT **Light shades, like vases, can become** *objets d'art,* **as this dainty blue ceramic shade with brass fixtures has.**

TOP **Industrial fixtures, like this utilitarian light, suit country's pared-down side. This style of shade throws a strong ray of light downward, providing task lighting as well as overall lighting. Find shades like this in secondhand outlets.**

light they get. It makes sense for rooms that are the home's social hubs, particularly during the day—the kitchen and living room—to bathe in the most light. The places where we just spend the beginning and end of the day, bedrooms and bathrooms, only need ambient light.

In the past, country cottage windows were tiny. Glass was expensive and let precious heat out, and cottage tenants spent most of their daytime hours outdoors anyway. Contemporary country's approach is to enlighten your home. Think windows. Bring in light wherever you can, punching skylights in the roof if possible. In urban houses, particularly older styles like turn-of-the-century row houses, installing a skylight above a flight of stairs creates a light well that lets light pour into the house.

ABOVE LEFT AND ABOVE **The eye adores visual rhythm, which is why lights naturally seem to look better in pairs. In the kitchen above, two industrial-style chrome lampshades flood the worktop below with light. Kitchen surfaces need task lights for food preparation. The light should be focused on, or angled toward, the countertop.**

Chandeliers add glamour to any setting. Even gigantic chandeliers seem to take up barely any space, as the light simply passes through their glass teardrops. Place them under skylights or in sunny rooms so the light can play on the glass, showing off the chandelier's curvy daytime silhouette. You can restore antique chandeliers, but modern reproduction versions can look just as alluring. Many old versions, such as the one opposite, have candleholders and, when lit, this glimmering centerpiece brings a soft, beautiful light to any room. Make sure the chandelier hangs low so candle smoke does not blacken your ceilings. If you want the candle look without fuss, invest in a modern version with artificial candles or a bulb in the center.

> Choose lights created from natural materials or old styles with a modern twist, like crystal teardrop chandeliers with modern bulbs.

Of course we all need artificial lights, but let your scheme mimic nature. Light constantly changes throughout the day, so install a system that throws out different highlights and shadows, from bright and breezy to dimmed and soothing. To create versatility, install dimmers and a variety of uplighters, downlighters, pendant lights, side lights, and wall lights.

Your lighting scheme also needs to reflect what activities will go on in each room. Make a list of the things you do and then find light solutions to suit. In the living room, for example, you'll need an overhead fixture to cast a general light over the room—put it on a dimmer switch and you can easily make this light bright for social occasions or dim and seductive for intimate talk. If your ceilings are low, avoid a long pendant light, as this draws the eye down and makes the ceiling appear even lower. Wall lights over paintings or ornaments will highlight your artworks, and you'll also require reading lights or floor lamps beside sofas if you like to unwind with the newspaper on the sofa at night.

In kitchens, you'll need task lighting to highlight work surfaces while you cook, as well as ambient light. Bedrooms, places for intimacy, mainly require atmospheric lighting, while bathrooms need a mix of subtle lighting for bathing and task lighting for shaving or applying makeup.

To echo the country theme, choose lights created from natural materials and fabrics, or choose old styles with a modern twist, like crystal teardrop chandeliers with modern bulbs. Styles with a nod to country sensibilities include ceramic lamps in organic shapes, wicker shades, and shades and bases married together from a mix of natural materials, like a wooden base with a floral cotton shade, or a wrought-iron base with an opaque paper shade.

Bulbs matter, too. For a mellow yellow light, choose incandescent or tungsten-filament bulbs. If you need more specific light for a task, try a halogen bulb. Avoid fluorescent bulbs, because their blue tinge feels cold-hearted and harsh. Daylight bulbs mimic the full spectrum of light.

The light of a flame is an age-old favorite. Faces look younger and softer in the gaze of firelight, so light candles whenever you can. For a rustic

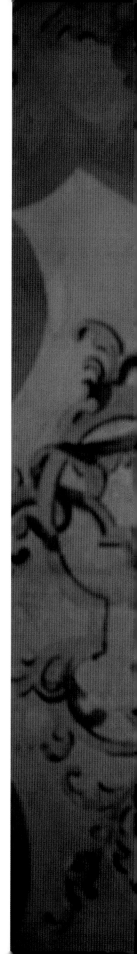

Make the most of natural light wherever you can. Windows connect you to the outside world, admitting light, air, and vistas. You could extend your current windows (ABOVE) or create double-height windows. These floor-to-ceiling doors (MAIN PICTURE) create a feeling of space, yet above them are even more large windows, so this room feels incredibly open, and almost part of the outdoor world. Inside, the white walls, pale furnishings, and concrete floors emphasize the light, making the room look even more spacious. An antique altar candlestick makes it feel like a sanctuary for the spirit.

BELOW LEFT **To wake yourself up gently, let natural light flood into your bedroom.**

BELOW RIGHT **Put seating by windows wherever you can. Here a ledge has been built in to the wall and covered with cushions to create a place to perch in the sunshine.**

BOTTOM **Skylights are an architect's quick-fix way of bringing maximum light into old country buildings, particularly barn conversions and dark cottages. In this remodeled barn, the small square panes of the skylights contrast with the large frames in the sliding doors below.**

ABOVE **With floor-to-ceiling windows, you can imagine that you are outside. The views feel like living murals. Where possible, keep window frames unadorned. This retains the country feeling of simplicity, but also looks pared-down and modern and allows in as much free-flowing light as possible.**

look, pop candles into old hurricane lamps or add dinner-party glamour by lighting long slender candles in an antique silver candelabra.

The opposite of light is shadow and darkness. We need to eschew full light at certain times, to create private spaces in our homes to sleep, bathe, and daydream. To provide privacy but let in some light, cover windows with materials that softly diffuse rays. Fabric pieces, like vintage lace shawls or loose-weave voile, will do the trick, or you can puncture natural cotton shades with evenly spaced holes. You could also half-cover the bottom of the window with old-fashioned fold-out shutters. While antique versions suit the look, there are plenty of contemporary styles made from wood or wicker. Otherwise, use contemporary country's favorites, Venetian or slatted wooden blinds. These versatile blinds can be half-shut, stopping people from peering in, but throwing bars of light across a room.

Most of us have centrally heated homes with radiators (OPPOSITE INSET) but a range (ABOVE AND LEFT) is a cast-iron country staple, providing a constant source of warmth from the kitchen. The oven is like a baker's brick oven, allowing you to cook succulent roasts and moist breads, and each compartment provides a different heat. The boiler plate is often quicker than a coffee-maker—a perfect place to brew a pot (LEFT).

A fireplace was once the heartland of every home. While not all of us have a fireplace, there's something about walking into a warm house that makes us feel instantly at home. Contemporary country heating is all about reviving old traditions, then reinterpreting them in a modern way.

heat

Modernity has turned our memory of open fires to ashes, although you can still light a log fire if you have a legal fireplace. "Real" fires are now banished from British cities after thick, soot-laden smog became lethal—on December 4, 1952, the "great smog of London" took the breath from 4,000 people. Now, thanks to smokeless fuels and secondary burners, home fires are ablaze again. So it's time to rekindle a contemporary country flame at home—the fire. If you're lucky enough to live in an area where wood-burning is permitted, choose woods with a sweet scent, like cedar,

FAR LEFT **An antique stove makes an elegant heating solution. Many come with clawed feet, ornate doors, relief patterns, and engraved details, which give them a refined, regal character all of their own.**

ABOVE LEFT **Wood doesn't have to be stacked in piles. For wood storage with a twist, an elegant bookshelf has been used to store logs.**

BELOW LEFT **Stoves with doors produce more heat than conventional fires, so if you need more warmth, consider installing a stove in your fireplace. This antique one, framed by a contemporary fireplace, is almost like an artwork.**

pine, and apple wood. If you live in a built-up area, you can enjoy the warmth of a naked flame with smokeless solid fuels like clean-burning coal, gas, or electric fires, or wood stoves with secondary burners (a second stove ignites and burns off solids created by the original fire, producing "clean" emissions).

If you open up an old chimney, have it properly inspected and swept before you strike a match. Make a beautiful frame for your fire; rediscover your home's original fireplaces if they are boxed in, or install reconditioned fireplaces, sourced from architectural salvage yards or secondhand dealers. For a modern fireplace, create a "hole in the wall," with simple, pared-back lines.

Stoves are a hot choice for looks and heat, as fires burn hotter when they are enclosed. There are many modern versions of the pot-belly stove, some of which even "float"

from a flue into the middle of a room. For a stove with history, buy an antique and reinstate an old beauty.

Whether you go for a stove or fireplace, make the most of it. In the living room, position your seating around the fireplace rather than the television, so you stare directly into the flames and bask in their bone-thawing warmth. The fireside is a great place to tell stories and talk, so provide plenty of cozy seats, a soft hearth rug, and lots of oversized cushions to accommodate your guests.

You'll also need plenty of accessories. Piles of logs stacked against a wall can look like living sculptures, and bring in wood's warmth and aromas. You could pile logs in old laundry baskets, wooden fruit cases, or tea chests. Source old-style coal scuttles, pokers, log baskets, bellows, and buckets from secondhand stores or markets. Buy a matching set or acquire an assortment of individual pieces.

A flickering, living flame brings so much more than just heat. As seen here, a fire injects life, light, and vitality, and acts as a people magnet. With a hearth at the heart of your home, visitors will feel at ease. The dark smooth flue of this modern stove looks youthful beside the thick ancient beams.

RIGHT Everyone is drawn to a fireplace, whether it's in use or not. If you can't use your fireplace, use it as a frame in which to display beautiful things. This handsome stone fireplace will provoke inspiring conversation.

If you can't rescue a disused fireplace, create a contemporary version, like this fire "shelf." Even when not in use, the black soot contrasts with the white walls to create visual drama.

In the living room, position seating around the fireplace so you stare directly into the flames and bask in their bone-thawing warmth.

The ancient Romans invented underfloor heating, but warm floors underfoot still feel indulgent today. Consider installing it if you're refurbishing or building a home, as it involves running wires or pipes underneath the floor, depending on whether the system is dry (electric) or wet (hot-water-based). If you choose tiles and flagstones, underfloor heating is a real boon in the winter months.

Other heating choices include standard radiators and convector or plinth heaters. They come in many colors and subtle modern designs, which you can hide away or expose. You could reconnect with old styles, like chunky, solid reconditioned radiators or reproduction versions.

Many large country homes throughout Europe have championed Aga ranges. The Aga employs the principle of heat storage, in which the range steadily transfers heat from its core to its ovens and hotplates. The stove is always on and ready to cook, while releasing a steady source of heat, making it perfect for big kitchens. Once they ran on oil and solid fuels, which makes original stoves quite costly to run, but you can now buy electric Agas. When an Aga is fired up, it releases heat and life into an entire home. Some systems also act as water heaters, and they're also good for drying laundry—in their heyday, they were regarded as a housewife's multitasking best friend.

Last, when you've created heat, save it. Insulate your home as efficiently as you can. Have insulating bats in the roof—a home without roof insulation in winter is really like a person going out without a hat. Fix insulation tape or hang thick curtains around your windows and drafty doorways, and double- or triple-glaze windows.

OPPOSITE **The essence of putting this look together is to combine and contrast nature's textures and materials. Wherever you can, pit them side by side for extra emphasis. Mix rough and smooth textures, like this weathered door and shiny glass tabletop, and soft matte surfaces with hard shiny surfaces, seen in the dyed sheepskin and chrome chair legs.**

RIGHT **This home is in the heart of the English countryside, as you can see from the interior's exposed wood skeleton. Yet with a retro chair and vintage silk cushion, this corner feels contemporary, chic, and almost urban.**

At the heart of contemporary country is a clash of elements. And, in many ways, the style is very eclectic and adaptable. "Contemporary" and "country," in fact, incorporate a whole gamut of looks. Country can be earthy and rustic, but also pretty and dainty, while contemporary can be hard-edged and hi-tech, but also comes with curvy, organic lines and rough weaves.

putting it all together

Contemporary country isn't a look you can just buy wholesale from one place—it's a compilation of your finds and fancies, and requires a little footwork. Some pieces may require a trip to your local salvage yard or a journey to a street market in France, or inspirational *objets trouvés* may come from a woodland walk. Sometimes it's

difficult to imprint exactly what you want on your mind's eye, so before you go out and about, take Polaroids of your rooms or, even better, capture images of them on a digital camera, which you can use as a reference. You could even take a leaf from a stylist's book, and create a pocket-sized mood book to take around with you. Stick in anything

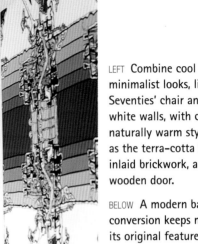

LEFT Combine cool minimalist looks, like this Seventies' chair and sleek white walls, with country's naturally warm style, such as the terra-cotta floors, inlaid brickwork, and wooden door.

BELOW A modern barn conversion keeps many of its original features, yet is updated with modern amenities, like the sleek contemporary stove right in the heart of the house. The modern red Fifties-style chair sits easily with a large antique kilim on the floor.

OPPOSITE This funky retro cocktail cabinet, adorned with sculptural glassware and a swanky red lamp, creates a chic corner in a rustic-style home.

that inspires you, like features from magazines, postcards, product brochures, internet printouts, swatches, paint cards, pressed flowers. Also include practical details such as the width of alcoves, if you are looking for an item to fit a particular space. Once you've got a picture of an item, you may be surprised at how easy it is to find. With your notebook at hand, it's harder to make costly and time-consuming mistakes. It's also a handy tool to help you with instant decision-making. In markets, if you wait, a piece may be snapped up by someone else. Weigh all prospective purchases up against your book, and you can determine quickly whether what you're about to buy will harmonize.

Sourcing the right mix of objects takes time. You'll find a lot of pieces at your local mall, as chic, very modern styles of furniture and ornaments give the look

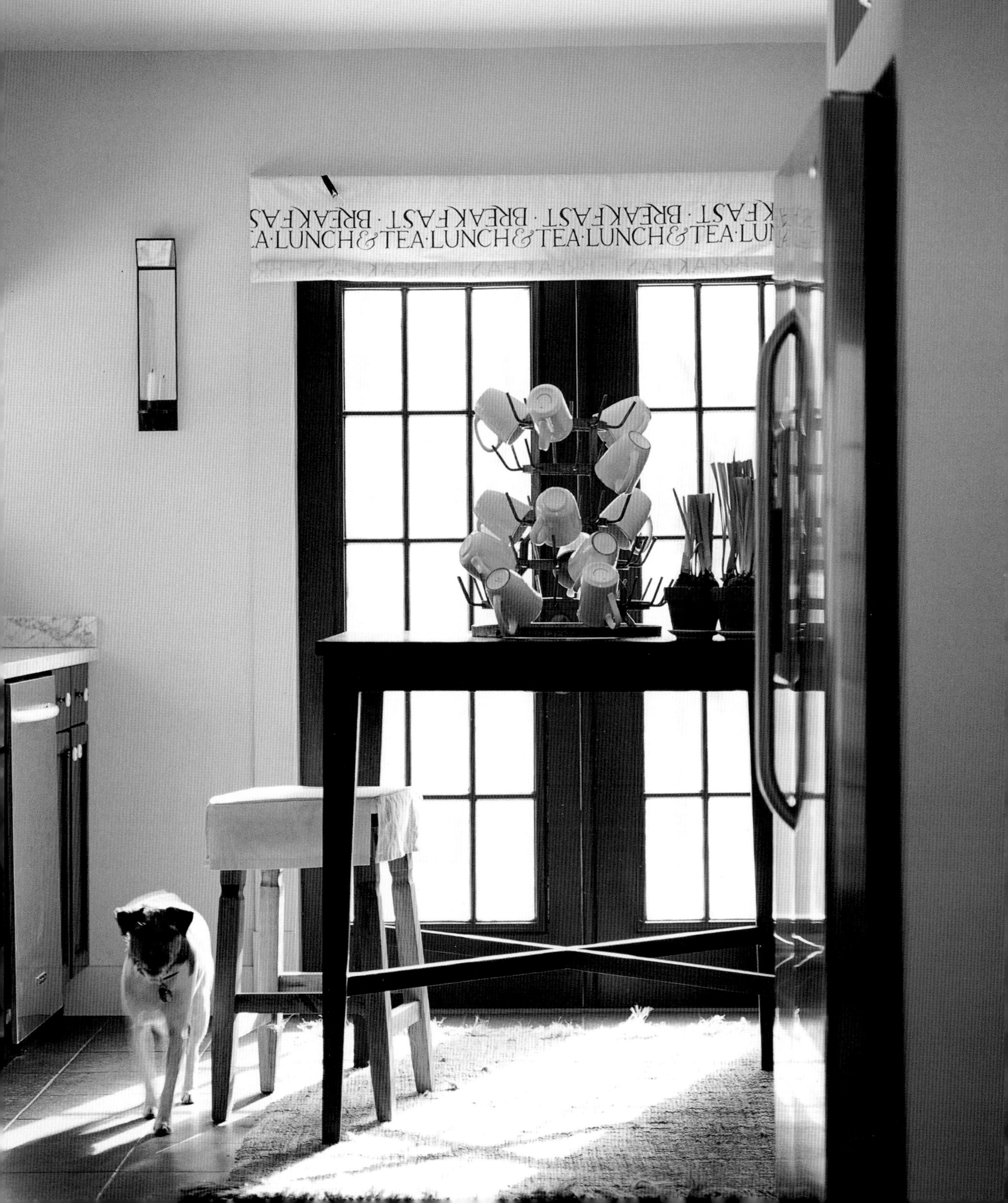
A·LUNCH & TEA·LUNCH & TEA·LUNCH & TEA·LUN

OPPOSITE **One of the look's key elements is light, and plenty of it. Here, a pair of French doors gives this kitchen a whole new extension in the summertime.**

RIGHT **Create a collision of old and new styles, like this rustic farmhouse table surrounded by retro modern chairs. Utilitarian light shades suit the table's raw, hard-working looks. To bring in light and garden views all year round, the owners added a wall of French doors. On the patio outside, there's a picnic table for summer dining.**

> You'll find modern pieces fashioned from key materials, like wood, glass, metal and polished steel. Team them with country's softer looks.

the contemporary edge it craves. So keep your eye out for pieces with interesting shapes that suit the style, such as chain-store reproductions of Verner Panton's curvy S chair, designed in the Sixties. You'll also find plenty of modern pieces fashioned from key contemporary materials, like wood, glass, metal, and polished steel. Just remember to team them with country's softer looks. For example,

you may discover a hard-edged black leather-and-chrome sofa that you love. If you pair it with a floral cushion, it will suit the look.

When considering how to arrange your home, you will probably want the public spaces (usually the living room and kitchen) to be the rooms with the most sunlight, while darker, quieter spaces can be home to your bedrooms and

The owners of this house fell in love with this huge hutch, the perfect size to fit their vast collection of old china, glassware, and linens. When they moved in, they enlarged the room to accommodate it. To bring light in, skylights were put in the roof, windows extended, and doors added to the back of the house.

"Create a little duality, mixing modern and traditional, rough textures with smooth, elegant with earthy, and hi-tech with rustic."

bathrooms. Don't be constrained by traditional dictates, however. If you love bathing in daylight, put the bathtub in the area that gets the most sun—this could be your conservatory, for example, or even your living room. You could also convert a spare bedroom into a bathroom, or put a shower on your outdoor patio. Fashion your home around your habits—and again, don't be afraid to be

unconventional. If you like an afternoon siesta, put a daybed or a sunlounger in your living room in a spot that catches the sun, so you can curl up.

Once indoors, strip back your floors and walls, and expose your home's bones and skin, such as raw plaster walls, old beams, or ancient brickwork. Floors are where we feel connected to the earth, so cover them in terra cotta, warm woods, or soft carpets. Unless you're going for the white-on-white look, keep floors in earthy, neutral shades. Cover your walls in wood, cork, paint, and paper, but again stick to cool neutrals, as these colors marry beautifully with modern stainless-steel finishes and pale wood floors. Warmer naturals combine well with cream and ecru in a more traditional interior.

With these neutral backdrops, bring in your beautiful things, starting with furniture. To achieve contemporary country style, you need to inject a little duality, mixing modern and traditional, rough textures with smooth, elegant with earthy, and hi-tech with rustic to create a look that's chic but grounded. It may take time to source the right pieces—the perfect sofa might be found in

ABOVE LEFT **Be inventive with storage. This old chest was used to store plans, and now is home to flatware and other kitchen utensils.**

ABOVE RIGHT **The top also makes an excellent work surface; meals are served here before being eaten at the large wood table.**

LEFT **Wicker baskets are a country staple for storing and collecting household items. Here a couple of baskets packed with linens are mounted onto a wall.**

Juxtapose old and new. These antique suitcases act as storage, and as an impromptu bedside table for a scented candle and Ingo Maurer light. This chic, contemporary bed has simple, strong lines and is adorned with beautiful linens in neutral colors. For simplicity's sake, there is no ornate headboard, just a clean, white wall for complete calm.

MAIN PICTURE This attic bedroom has an air of romance. A dyed mosquito net is draped over the bed, while two old army trunks reside at its foot. In the background, two army blankets are rolled up and held together with thick woven belts.

INSET Create small pockets of detail beside large objects, like this collection of nighttime necessities by a grandiose gilt-framed red headboard.

RIGHT A sequined cushion and a lace throw add a twist of femininity to this otherwise naked room. Instead of a central pendant light, the owner has chosen a modern classic, the Castiglioni "Arco" lamp, to inject modernity into an otherwise traditional room.

desperate need of a makeover at an architectural salvage yard. Styles such as boxy modern pieces, Thirties' club chairs, or Chesterfield sofas don't date, and may just need a little bit of effort to mend, repaint, or restore.

Then it's time for the details. To help create visual contrasts, put these smaller, finer items beside large plain objects. For example, put a cluster of pebbles on a table beside your sofa or some fine china teacups on a large thick bookshelf made of weathered woods. Create collections of the things you find or cherish—Fifties' cake stands, retro glassware, or vintage leather suitcases—and put them on display.

As in nature, a contemporary country home changes with the seasons, particularly when it comes to soft furnishings. In the summer, opt for light, bright fabrics for cushion covers and throws, and keep vases brimming with wild flowers. In winter, you'll appreciate thick, plump, soft cushion covers, sheepskins on the floor, and wool blankets.

There isn't an exact recipe for creating the look, because it's an organic process. Follow the advice of Ilse Crawford, who says in her book *Home is Where The Heart Is?*: "There is only one rule. Leave space for change, a place for passing passions, for something else to come along."

spaces

A contemporary country kitchen is hi-tech, yet down to earth. Here mod cons, like the TV, double sink, and huge oven, sit comfortably with an enormous wooden table, rough plaster walls, and thick wooden chopping boards. Large skylights provide light all day long. With a homey mix of country and modern, this cooking-dining room is the perfect space for entertaining guests.

cooking & eating

Certain elements will always define a country kitchen. It possesses a generous, warm sense of abundance; it's clean, but not sterile; it's a working kitchen, full of local foods and homemade produce; and, most importantly, it's a people magnet. Contemporary country kitchens blend these traditional features with modern conveniences to create a warm, inviting place where people are welcome to cook, eat, and enjoy life.

While some of us might get misty-eyed over farmhouse kitchens, they really weren't all peaches and cream. There was an endless round of firewood-fetching, hand-washing, chopping, polishing, plucking, steaming, stewing, kneading, and pickling to be done. A rustic brick floor was hard to clean with wicker brooms, and keeping the fire going briskly in the hearth was a time-consuming task. Luckily, that's where modern machinery—spacious fridges, automatic breadmakers, dishwashers, and electric ovens—has taken over from the rustic reality of days gone by.

The key in creating a contemporary country kitchen is to find a balance between rustic style—raw materials such as granite countertops, wooden chopping boards, generously large pots, and marble pastry boards and rolling pins—and modern looks. Too many hi-tech gadgets and cool, minimalist whites or swathes of stainless steel make a kitchen appear cold, clinical, and sterile.

The contemporary country kitchen needs to be utilitarian and uncomplicated, with ample storage and preparation space, hard-wearing natural surfaces, plenty of light and air, generous waste and recycling space, and sturdy utensils made of wood and metal rather than plastic.

One of the components that makes a country kitchen inviting is simply the food itself. There's nothing quite like seeing its vibrant colors and smelling its pungent aromas. Kitchens with no food on display seem starved, so make sure your storage is a healthy mix of closed cabinets and open shelving. Decorate your shelves and benches with colorful foods, including large jars of dried goods, overflowing fruit bowls, and garlands of garlic. To add to the feeling of abundance, grow aromatic leafy herbs on your sunny windowsills, such as peppermint, thyme, lemon balm, basil, cilantro, parsley, and pots of rosemary. If you have a patio near the kitchen door, rosemary and lavender can grace big pots there.

Base your kitchen layout around the main activities of food preparation, cooking, serving, and eating. Many of us have now dispensed with the formal dining room, knocking through walls to create one generously sized area. The

ABOVE **With a view onto the garden, this informal eating space is the perfect place to sip a hot coffee by day, but with a tablecloth transforms to a dining area at night.**

ABOVE RIGHT **The molded wood chairs flanking this shiny, smooth dining table are modern classics. Behind the table is an enormous hearth with cut wood at the ready.**

business of preparing to eat is no longer separated from eating itself. You could even consider integrating your living space with the kitchen or knocking down a hall wall to create one large living and dining space.

The kitchen has always been regarded as the heart of the home, so make it as welcoming as possible, bringing in light, air, and space. As with your other rooms, spend some time in your kitchen before deciding on the color scheme and layout. Most of us gravitate toward a tried-and-tested U- or L-shaped kitchen, but don't be constrained by tradition. Create a cooking and eating area that works for you. You may like a U-shape, for example, but with an island in the middle for storage and food preparation.

If you've got a small kitchen, keep the overall look light and bright. Consider a color scheme of off-white (pure white can look too sterile) and maximize the light with plenty of reflective surfaces like stainless steel and glass. Avoid low-hanging rails with dangling pots and pans or pendant lights, as they tend to make the ceiling look lower. If you're particularly space-pressed, you could always employ a foldaway table on hinges.

Choose large appliances such as your refrigerator, freezer, and dishwasher to suit the look. For a seamless appearance, hide them behind built-in doors that match your cabinets. Most family homes demand a big fridge, and there are many stylish modern designs available, so this is one piece of kitchenware you may want to display. You can buy reproduction versions of classic retro fridge designs in a huge array of colors, or you could select a stainless-steel model that's chic and hi-tech.

Again, with your oven, you can choose a freestanding retro style and make it into a feature, or buy a model that blends in seamlessly with your other furniture. While gas cooktops are a cook's dream, if you don't cook a lot you could choose an electric version with a streamlined glass cover that looks like part of a run of work surfaces.

When choosing furnishings for your kitchen, you can either opt for freestanding choices (perfect if you plan

Create eating spaces that work with the way you live. Here a kitchen breakfast bar makes an informal spot to have a quick bite in the morning, while a round glass table offers a more formal dining area for the evening.

to move house again) or built-in furniture. Many freestanding country-style choices—like wooden food trolleys, butcher's blocks, hutches, and pantries—are widely available in shops and are also resurfacing at auction, so buy these for an authentic rustic look. Otherwise, build in units with a country ethos, opting for solid, robust materials that will withstand the daily hardships of kitchen labor. When building your furniture, combine chic contemporary and traditional country styles. Choose units hewn from weathered woods, paired with stylish polished stainless-steel handles, or go for sandblasted glass-fronted cupboards with sturdy wooden handles. Avoid using composite board, as it has a short life.

The most important surface in any kitchen is the floor. It has to be easy to clean, nonslip, and handsome, which is

ABOVE LEFT Hide some kitchenware behind closed doors and put your favorites on show. This treasure trove includes grain sifters, china jugs, olive oil bottles, an ice bucket, and more.

ABOVE RIGHT Contemporary country kitchens feel simple, but abundant. While this one contains modern equipment like the blender, it also has time-honored country elements such as the butler's sink and a generous bread bin.

quite a tall order. Country's traditional coverings—stone, wood, natural linoleum, and tiles—can be expensive, but will withstand spills, grease, heat, and heavy appliances and still look good after many years.

Counters are the next most utilized surface, so choose a material that's good-looking, hard-working, and resilient. Granite is one of the most expensive options, but it is the toughest of all work surfaces. You can cut, chop, and place

If space is tight, hang a fold-down table on the wall. This hutch harks back to its ancestors, but the floating shelf above gives it a modern spin. Glassware and china help preserve the feeling of space.

Even urbanites long for home cooking from country kitchens, so you'll find wire egg baskets, wicker storage, bread bins, and more in chain stores.

hot pans on it without worrying. Other seductive stone options include beautiful slate and limestone. These are eye-catching but not as hardy as granite; they can be porous and stain. Before buying, ask your supplier about protective varnishes and keep a large wooden chopping board close by for your food preparation work. Marble also marks, but its cool texture makes it a pastry chef's best friend, so keep a marble board as part of your kitchen tools. Warm-to-touch wood is an old country favorite, but only use hardwoods such as maple, beech, or cherry, which

are waterproof and hard-wearing. Thick tiles are another option, but bear in mind that you may need to have them professionally installed. The grouting between the tiles must be seamless, or food can get caught there. If heavy pots fall on them, the tiles can crack, so keep a few spares for emergency repairs. Last, for a chic contemporary look, opt for stainless-steel counters. While it does last the distance, stainless steel can become scratched over time, so once again, use a large chopping board for food preparation to protect the surface.

THIS PAGE A black-painted floor, pale mushroom walls, and mauve ceiling provide a canvas for this wooden farmhouse table flanked by industrial-style seats.

OPPOSITE Black-and-white architectural details create a sense of visual drama in this large informal dining area, linked to the living room by a graceful archway.

If you have a small dining area or a room with a low ceiling, a glass tabletop is the answer. Light passes freely through it or reflects from it, so it won't make the room seem even smaller. Reinvent modern dining chairs if you find them. These Seventies' chairs were given a new lease on country life with oatmeal-colored covers.

RIGHT Industrial style suits country's raw edges, which is why the look is often at home in urban loft apartments. Here old china nestles on metal shelving, while old factory lamps light up a farmhouse-style table.

BELOW RIGHT Glossy black cabinets stand in stark contrast to this kitchen's exposed wooden beams and tiled floor, yet seem quite at home. The retro Seventies' black-leather chairs and the chrome and glass table give this old farmhouse a contemporary twist.

If you have a modern kitchen, country accessories will count. Displaying items of old-style or vintage kitchenware adds authenticity to the look. For a start, put large pots and pans on display. You can hang them from a rail using butcher's hooks, or suspend a large rack above your sink. You'll find old enamel cooking pots, copper pans, and cast-iron versions in secondhand outlets. Other details also enhance the look. Source butler's sinks with big pillar faucets, reproduction Fifties-style fridges, or an old Aga or pot-bellied stove to contrast with your hi-tech toaster, blender, and waffle iron.

Some traditional kitchen tasks such as making jams and preserves are becoming increasingly rare, but you can still find handsome jars, strainers, and large preserving pots secondhand. Keep your eye out for other items like old wooden bread bins, flour tins, sugar canisters, and cookie tins, and put them on display.

Since even hardcore urbanites long for the nostalgia of home cooking from country kitchens, you'll find plenty of wire egg baskets, wicker storage baskets, bread bins, and more in chain stores and

specialized kitchen stores. Look out for pieces that suit the style; for example, a big wooden or granite pestle and mortar or giant wooden salt and pepper grinders.

Eating fresh, home-cooked food with family and friends is one of life's great pleasures. Yet in our fast-paced society, it's not always easy to sit down to eat together. With people coming and going, the trick is to create flexible dining options. If your family doesn't sit down together for breakfast, you could create a diner-style area where those eating on the run can perch on high stools. If you find yourselves drawn to the living room at the end of the day, strew cushions around a low-level coffee table and dine in Arabic style.

BELOW **With its relaxed seating, this dining area feels very informal. The table has been painted black in contrast to the purity of the white, high-backed chairs. At night, a large hanging fixture provides lighting to dine by, while by day plenty of light floods in from the oversized windows.**

ABOVE **This kitchen's storage is tucked away in cupboards with push catches and drawers. With a stainless-steel fridge, Dualit toaster, and stylish kettle, the look is minimalist, right down to the wall-mounted faucets. A fruit bowl and nature-inspired modern art on the wall bring its pared-back lines down to earth. Stainless-steel work lamps light the surfaces below.**

Lure your family or friends with delicious fresh food, a beautifully set table and the promise of good conversation. Buy an enormous table so everyone feels welcome. Choose with care, however. Wooden tables feel warm to touch and lean on, while glass tables work well in smaller interiors. Remember that natural materials are the most hard-wearing (and most kitchen furniture is heavily used). For more on buying dining furniture, see page 29.

A well-dressed table is inviting. For a country feel, source large, thick plates from flea markets—they don't have to

Two low-hanging, industrial-style pendant lamps provide a wash of light at night for this large, modern dining room. With warm creams, wicker weaves, and brushed flat aluminum, the color scheme feels tranquil, calm, and sedate—perfect for dining. A contemporary fruit platter crowns the table, while ripe fruits bring in a splash of color.

This basement kitchen is full of zest. The cupboards are just the right shade of orange to marry with the glossy wood floors and dark beams. Two big hampers provide more food storage. They're parked beneath a rustic table, designed to give the chef ample food preparation space. Lights attached to the beam just out from the bench are angled to light the kitchen countertops.

RIGHT **Every work surface in this kitchen is illuminated with dainty pendant lights. The red–white–blue color scheme is an offbeat choice for a kitchen, but works effortlessly. The white roof and the light blue bench offset the deep red on the far kitchen wall. The owner has kept some ceiling beams exposed and painted the rest a fresh white. This delineates the space, marking where the kitchen ends and the stairs begin.**

If your family doesn't breakfast together, create a diner-style area where those eating on the run can perch on stools.

match. You could buy a collection with floral decorations, or plates with stripes around the edge. Markets are a great source of secondhand flatware, particularly lovely old silver pieces and knives with bone handles (don't put these in the dishwasher)—and again, you don't have to find a set. Simply buy a selection of similar sizes. To go one step further, look out for beautiful pieces like silver or glass salt and pepper shakers, silver serving dishes, china gravy boats, and ornate trivets.

Cover your table with a beautiful cloth. You could use an antique linen sheet, an old curtain made from vintage fabric, a silk sari as a table runner or, for a rustic look, sew a cloth from a patchwork of old linen dishtowels. You can find linen napkins in flea markets, or make your own by cutting up a linen sheet. Present them in antique napkin rings. Instead of a conventional flower arrangement, pop single gerbera heads in Moroccan tea glasses down the table or rose heads in dainty teacups. The area will need light, so make it rustic style. You could install an overhead pendant light with a dimmer switch for flexible lighting that can be turned up for cleaning or dimmed for soft lighting that's conducive to conversation. To dine by country-style candlelight with a modern twist, put tea lights in hurricane lamps or long candles in antique candelabras, or dot thick altar candles down the center of the table.

This beautiful living room has been inspired by nature. Two enormous chandeliers hanging low from ribbons crown the room. Beside the chaise longue draped in an antique sheet, there's an ornate coffee table, perfectly placed. In the corner, there's a long-legged painted table, with delicate hand-painted Moroccan tea glasses on top.

living

Contemporary country living rooms are down-to-earth and practical spaces, yet when decked out in natural materials, they become luxurious and comfortable. The look can accommodate all the demands made on a living room throughout the day. For entertaining guests to a place for the children to play, a contemporary country living room fulfills everyone's dreams.

This is a room where a lot of different activities collide. For many of us, games, hobbies, children, and friends all coexist in one large living space. Sometimes it's an impromptu dining room, sometimes a place just to sit and read the newspaper, sometimes it's a playground.

The three elements to be considered In any living room are comfort, function, and style. Each element can then be given a contemporary country spin. In many ways, this room is where the style can hit its stride. Nature provides almost all the materials we need to be comfortable, and since most of them are robust and hard-wearing, they're also very functional. Natural materials are handsome even in their unadorned state, so with a little styling can look stunning. Also, by incorporating the other, less tangible, elements of country style—space, light, and air—the living room feels like somewhere we can be at home with nature.

If you can, choose the room in the house that catches the most sunshine as your main living area. Could your master bedroom, for example, be a better living room? Whichever room you choose, make sure it's got plenty of windows. Consider integrating the space with the kitchen or knocking down the hall wall to create one large, welcoming space. Last, consider architectural renovations and create connections with the outside world wherever you can with large floor-to-ceiling windows or French doors.

LEFT With children's game boxes stacked to make a side table for an anglepoise lamp, this room is very much a family room. Almost the whole clan can perch on this long, Chesterfield-style deep-buttoned sofa. An old kilim adorns the floor.

Employ visual trickery to play with the room's shape. Remember, light colors recede, making spaces appear larger, while darker colors advance, causing rooms to look smaller and cozier. To make the ceiling seem higher, paint a dark color up to your chest height and then use a lighter color up to the ceiling. Painting the ceiling in an even paler shade will make it look higher still. Don't forget you can also visually iron out an oddly shaped room with a pale monochrome scheme, which makes all surfaces seem perfectly flat. While most contemporary rooms need a pale neutral scheme to expand the space, if you have a small living room, you could always go for an intimate look and create a den-like feel by painting your room a plush, deep color, like burgundy or midnight blue.

When it comes to decorating, start by bringing nature's earthy looks to the room's largest surfaces: its floors and walls. Natural flooring ages gracefully, so choose flagstones, terra-cotta tiles, wooden boards, or soft pure wool carpets. Since living rooms are where you entertain

THIS PICTURE White walls and painted wood floors make a simple canvas for sophisticated furniture and furnishings. There is a mix of practical and romantic lighting in the room, from the large floor uplighter providing a wash of light to an antique candelabra.

LEFT One of the most striking features in this room is the fluted column, which instead of supporting a statue displays a curvaceous lamp. The lamp base is clear glass, filled with maple-syrup-colored liquid. Instead of a pendant light, which would draw the eye down and make the ceiling look lower, the lamp provides overall light for the room and becomes a sculptural centerpiece.

RIGHT This house has two living areas: through the door is a reading room, with a stereo and bookshelves, while the nearer room is a more public area. A small posy of flowers and tall glass candlesticks add a touch of elegance. The antique wood floor is softened with a rattan rug (foreground) and a sheepskin (background).

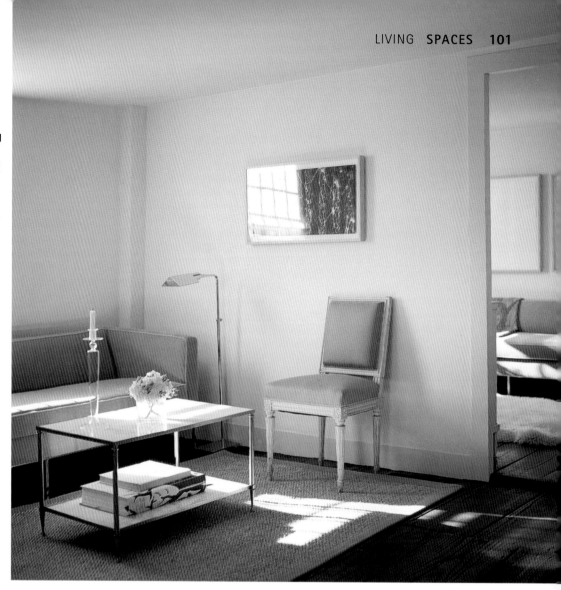

Since the number of your visitors will vary, it's a wise idea to have flexible seating options. These include single chairs, floor cushions, and stools.

guests, you'll want to give your coveted things center stage. Turn your walls into canvases with a neutral or monochrome color scheme. You can also create coverings for your walls with neutral natural materials like wood paneling, terra-cotta tiles, or luxurious leather. For a simple smooth canvas, use chalky organic paint.

All living rooms end up being arranged around a focal point. For many, it's the TV. Yet while most of us like a bit of TV, try to avoid making it the room's eye magnet.

Encase it in a beautiful cabinet with doors, or put it out of the way on a stool with wheels, so you can easily move it into view when you feel like watching it.

If your fireplace is the focal point, fashion it into a feature worthy of its status. You could go for a contemporary hole-in-the-wall fireplace or an ornate antique version. A restored or modern stove is equally magnetizing (for more on heating, see pages 62–67). Otherwise, adapt the unused space so it conveys warmth and beauty. Its stark,

To bring in light to this living space, the owners have punched skylights and added floor-to-ceiling windows in the stairway wall. To harness the light, the walls are painted a reflective white, the floor is glossy, and the furnishings are covered in cream muslin. A chandelier seems to float above the room.

ABOVE **Quirky natural elements give this room an earthy, original country look. Orchids are displayed in a big black rubber pot, a deer skull and antlers adorn the walls, and a battered old leather pouffe provides an extra seat. To promote conversation, the seating has been arranged around a contemporary "hole in the wall" fireplace instead of the TV, which is tucked away on a floating shelf.**

soot-black backdrop could be a plain canvas for a huge display of fresh flowers, altar candles of various sizes, or a sculpture. Accessorize your mantelpiece with eye-catching pieces. Adorn it with beautiful objects, photographs, or artworks, and eschew keys and mail. Crown your fireplace with your most-loved artwork or a large mirror. If your style is minimalist, a hearth rug in front of the fire will soften the overall look and add a feeling of warmth. A flokati rug or white sheepskin or goatskin will fit in with this style, or for the more traditionally minded, an aged kilim or Turkish rug blends in well.

If this room is used for everything from relaxing to entertainment, you'll need to create layered lighting here (a dimmer switch on your main light will be helpful). Your central light will provide overall lighting for the

room but, even more important, it will be one of the first details your visitors see, so make it an eye-catching feature. You could choose a glamorous traditional or contemporary chandelier, a big moon-sized paper light shade, or a large wicker light. As this room is where you entertain, think about lighting options with sparkle—from glamorous crystal chandeliers to strings of fairy lights or a twinkling disco ball. If you like to read, you'll need floor lamps or adjustable side lights for reading. Bring attention to your artworks and *objets trouvés*, too, by the use of picture lights and spotlights.

Of course, you'll also need plenty of natural light. Windows connect us with the outdoors. Nothing rivals watching a clear winter's night sky when you're star-gazing from a sofa beneath a run of skylights or listening to the soothing sound of rain beating on the windows. Wherever you can, extend your current windows or create skylights to bring in nature's daily weather and light shows. Throw them open to let fresh air inside. To create more light from your current windows, scrub them till they are spotless and cut back foliage to let in precious golden light.

Many of the activities in the living room, like listening to music, watching TV, talking, and reading, are carried out in chairs or with your feet up. So as bed is to bedroom, sofa is to living room. The bigger the sofa, the better. With big sofas, you can stretch out or accommodate more visitors.

For sofa covers, natural fabrics are the most hard-wearing. Read more about the advantages of a leather sofa on page 26. Cottons, linens, canvases, and wool blends look just as handsome as leather, and these covers are easy

OPPOSITE In an open-plan space, this modular Seventies-style sofa delineates the living area. The TV, sited on a plank of wood supported by plastic storage bins, and the robust stove are the room's focal points. While the black leather seating dominates the color scheme, there are accents of orange on the modern classic chairs (foreground) and a pouffe (background).

LEFT While seated indoors, this owner can contemplate a river view. For summer, there is a rustic-style seating area on the deck with two stripped sawn logs and a contemporary table.

THIS PICTURE Two sets of floor-to-ceiling sliding doors mean rooms can be enclosed or opened, depending on the weather.

to clean. When choosing a sofa, make sure its color and shape suit the room and the kind of guests you're expecting. In a room with high ceilings, you could easily have a grand, large, high-backed sofa—it won't detract from the space. However, if you've got small children but want a light-colored sofa, a sofa in white or cream leather is one of the best options. If there are any accidents, you can simply wipe it down.

If you still like the shape of an old sofa that has seen better days, you can easily change its character. A good-quality cotton throw will hide a multitude of sins. You could also try an embroidered bedspread, a checked tablecloth, two vintage linen sheets sewn together, or a patchwork of old plaid throws. To disguise a dated shape, you can always add a folded quilt on the arms or across the back in the center. If you have an old-fashioned chaise longue, try covering it in a chic modern fabric.

Since the number of your visitors will vary, flexible seating options are a wise idea. These include single chairs, floor cushions, pouffes, and stools. Old wicker chairs, metal garden chairs, leather- or corduroy-covered beanbags, rocking chairs, and generously large armchairs all sit amicably side by side. With these items, you can move the living room around and reconfigure it as needed. Otherwise, when not in use, a stool is a handy side table, and a pouffe can become a comfortable footrest.

LEFT All the colors in this living room are neutrals, but the space is brought to life by an array of textures. The tongue-and-groove ceiling mirrors the painted wooden boards on the floor. To soften the look, a rattan rug cloaks the floor, while big chunky knitted rugs and coarse linen cushions sit on linen-covered sofas. A low-hanging basketweave pendant provides a dappled light for the entire room.

> Cushions accessorize a sofa like a stylish belt lifts a pair of jeans. Cushions can create a contrast to your color scheme, particularly if it's a fairly neutral one.

Cushions accessorize a sofa or a set of chairs like a stylish belt lifts a pair of jeans. Any plain-Jane sofa will instantly get a facelift. Cushions on sofas can create a contrast to your color scheme, particularly if it's a fairly neutral one. For example, if your walls, sofas, and floor are in mushrooms and browns, your cushions could be a mix of burnt orange, plum, and cream. For a sedate feel, place cushions side by side in subtle shades of the same colorway, like slate gray to sky blue. As in the natural world, a hodgepodge of pattern sometimes looks stunning, such as cushions with red-and-white striped covers, florals, and paisleys, or geometric-shaped cushions. Oversized cushions with covers made from thicker materials like suede, canvas, and leather can also make seating for extra guests.

"If your fireplace is the focal point, make it worthy of its status. You could go for a contemporary hole-in-the-wall fireplace or an ornate antique."

RIGHT **This barn conversion is simply breathtaking. The owners have exposed the barn's ancient skeleton, while adding in modern architectural elements like big skylights, glass doors, and a huge** fireplace with an enormous polished flue. The owner is a collector of modern classic furniture, seen in the wood and black leather lounger by Charles and Ray Eames (on the rug) and other retro pieces.

Every living room needs a low coffee table to hold things like books and magazines. Low tables also serve as impromptu informal dining tables and places for your guests to rest their drinks. For a rustic feel, choose a table made from wood, glass, or metal. You could make your own by sawing the legs off an old farmhouse table, or place a piece of beveled glass on top of a pair of thick railroad ties. Smaller side tables are also handy for sofa dwellers to park their coffee cups and reading or writing materials. Keep them in line with the theme by choosing a nest of wooden stacking tables, old school desks, or occasional tables. For a modern twist, plexiglass and glass tables look like they're barely there and take up little visual space.

Rooms with many uses demand good storage, particularly if the room is sometimes used as a children's playroom. To make sure toys don't prevent you from relaxing at the end of the day, provide plenty of storage for play things to vanish into, but choose something in contemporary country style, like an enormous tea chest or vintage leather suitcases stacked side by side.

Other large storage alternatives are bedroom drawers, antique armoires, and traditional or contemporary wooden sideboards. Once deemed old-fashioned, sideboards are making a comeback—old designs are often exquisitely crafted, with carved details on legs, doors, and knobs, hewn from woods that are now protected, like mahogany, ebony, and teak. If they're a little derelict, either sand and re-varnish them or paint them to suit your room. You can also buy streamlined contemporary sideboards. A modern take on large storage is to create an entire wall of storage: extend a wall by a couple of feet and build in flush-fronted cupboards with floor-to-ceiling, push-catch doors painted in the same shade as the

room, so the whole unit blends in. If you have an oddly shaped room, creating areas of storage is a smart way of squaring off corners and alcoves.

Every living room needs an abundance of growing things to bring in energy and vitality. Include plenty of greenery in the form of potted plants, shrubs, and even small trees. If you're forgetful or often away, choose plants that survive with minimal water, like aloe vera, yucca trees, and cacti. Otherwise, pick plants that look good as well as detox the air (see page 19 for varieties). Fresh flowers add scent and color, so make sure you always have a newly picked bunch on your mantelpiece or coffee table.

If you can, try to amalgamate indoor and outdoor areas. That way your living room will seem to go on forever in the summer and become a roofed extension of the garden.

You could consider building a glass conservatory over your patio, if you have one, creating a place that almost feels like outdoors all year round. When connecting outdoor and indoor spaces, go for an integrated look, extending a wooden living-room floor out onto a wooden deck or flagstones onto a stone or tile patio.

In summer, or whenever the weather permits, decamp outside and make alternative living rooms in your garden, complete with cooking and seating areas. Create small hideaways where you can sit, mediate, listen to nature, and watch the natural world go by. Pick a sheltered position under a canopy of tree branches, or a secluded area near the house. For seating, you can either choose weatherproof garden furniture made from sustainable tropical hardwoods or wrought iron, or you can build in

Bring the outdoors in. In summer, these door-windows slide back to open this sunken lounge directly onto a patio (RIGHT). A whole wall of windows opens out, so the room feels part of the outdoor world, with its view of fields. The warm tones of wood on the exterior and interior blend this countryside home seamlessly with its environment. Inside the living room, the light mustard-colored daybed is the perfect place to settle down, grab a book from the built-in shelves behind, and relax. On the wooden table, a cut-off ostrich egg and other items add detail.

boat-style seating that blends seamlessly with your decks, and which, if it has hinged tops, can also double as outdoor storage (you could put your outdoor accessories here, like barbecue equipment, charcoal, and umbrellas). Otherwise, go for the simplest option and place picnic blankets made from old blankets or old comforters on the ground, scattering oversized cushions around them to sit or lie on.

Shift your dining area outdoors, too, and eat al fresco under the stars. Make sure the area is ambient and inviting, illuminating your garden's beautiful plants with uplights, spotlights, and "starlights" (string fairy lights in a tree to create a sparkling grotto). Flares and candle flames also bring light into the garden, so dot them around in hurricane lamps or small glass jars. For fragrant dining, plant an abundance of scented flowers that release their perfume at night, like honeysuckle and jasmine, around your dining area.

We all love food cooked on a flame, and modern barbecues make cooking outdoors as easy as pie. Simply flick a switch or light a match to revive the tradition of spit-roasting meats and vegetables. And, for dessert, you can throw a banana filled with chocolate wrapped in foil into the burning embers and devour it as soon as the chocolate has melted.

ABOVE **Contemporary seating looks quite at home in a country setting. These funky wire-framed chairs with interchangeable cotton covers flank old garden tables.**

LEFT **In summer, create living spaces outdoors, contemporary country style. Even in the winter, this gorgeous swimming pool in the south of France creates a haven among the trees. The distressed door and stone wall belie the modern interior behind them.**

OPPOSITE **In your outside space, create places to sit and enjoy nature. This two-seater bench, covered in distressed paint, provides a suitably rustic perch with a garden view.**

Contemporary country style
extends well to bathrooms.
Here modern fixtures and a
cream wet-room enclosure
contrast with the rustic
looks of an old wooden
wall. An adjustable arm
lets the bather choose the
height of the shower head.

bathing

The bathroom is probably the only room in your home where you can lock out the world, disrobe, and relax. Here we can luxuriate in water, cleanse our bodies, and rejuvenate our flagging spirits.

Once we bathed in lakes, rivers, and springs. Later, pans of water were heated on the fire, and the whole family used them to wash in front of the flames. Now, with the advent of modern plumbing, we have plenty of options. Bathing is one of life's luxuries, so indulge your body and spirit.

If possible, apply country's coveted elements of light and space. Instead of relegating the bathroom to the smallest, darkest room in the home, renovate the spare bedroom or create an open-plan area connected to your bedroom.

If your bathroom is compact, however, employ visual trickery to make it appear bigger. Bring in natural light with skylights and reflect it around the room with pale, glossy surfaces and strategically placed mirrors. With artificial lighting, dot spotlights around the perimeter of the ceiling and the whole room will seem larger.

For the flooring, choose natural materials that are kind to feet, such as wood, nonslip tiles, slate (check with your supplier for a suitable variety), or carpet. For walls, you'll need a paint that's waterproof and able to withstand humidity, so choose a variety with a microporous coating,

ABOVE RIGHT **This bathroom is bought to life with a large window. Choose sandblasted glass panes for privacy, or string up a white cotton curtain. To prevent the curtain from getting mildew, use a waterproof fabric spray and make sure there's adequate ventilation.**

BELOW RIGHT **Many bathrooms are small, dark rooms, so keep the color scheme light and bright. This owner has used white tiles on the walls, built-in sinks, and a shower area to maximize the light. A monochrome look such as this one also helps iron out irregularly shaped rooms.**

For a contemporary twist, mount the tub on reclaimed railroad ties, paint the sides deep chocolate brown, or paper it with vintage wallpaper.

which allows the walls to breathe. You could also finish your walls in an aromatic, naturally waterproof wood paneling such as Japanese cypress, cedar, or breathable untreated cork.

If your bathtub is going to take center stage in the bathroom, choose one that's beautiful to look at. Old French-style rolltop tubs suit the look. Many companies produce reproductions, or you could source a vintage piece. Re-enameling a bathtub is a costly exercise, so choose one that's already been restored. For a contemporary twist, mount the tub on reclaimed railroad ties, paint the sides deep chocolate brown, or paper it with vintage wallpaper.

ABOVE LEFT **This bathroom employs contemporary country in a quirky way. Without the exposed wood beams, zebra-print bathmat, deep sink, and the artwork portraying a rural idyll, it would look dull.**

ABOVE RIGHT **Place your tub under large windows or a skylight so you can enjoy a sky view as you bathe. This modern tub is mounted on old wooden railroad ties. Kind to bare feet, a woolen mat beside the bathtub provides an elegant nonslip surface for the bather to step out onto.**

The Japanese, who have more than 20,000 natural springs to bathe in, are bathing aficionados. They favor wooden tubs, which retain heat well and smell aromatic when wet. You can now buy Zen-style square or rectangular tubs made from tropical woods like iroko, cedar, and rubber woods. Square sitz-style tubs are also a good choice for pint-sized bathrooms. Consult your supplier about upkeep—detergents strip the wood of its natural oils, so use wood soap instead.

For a country spin, avoid the traditional three-piece set. Instead, opt for original looks. You could marry an old ceramic sink with a Victorian-style toilet and a rolltop bathtub, or create a beautiful

A country-style door with an iron latch provides a rustic entrance to a modern toilet and laundry area. This owner has injected a rustic feel in the details, such as the wooden box for toilet paper, glass jug of flowers, and a shelf with an assortment of jars and vases.

LEFT **To create a Zenlike calm, this bathroom is clean-lined and simple. The tub has a smooth concrete surround, while the window frame is left almost naked to let in plenty of light. The bathtub is perfectly sited beneath the windows, which provide ventilation and a source of sweet fresh air for the bather.**

Put a chair in your shower to enjoy a deluge of water and get on with the business of cleaning your body. If you like to bathe, hark back to the Japanese tradition of thoroughly cleaning yourself first, so you don't have to do a thing when you relax in a steamy tub of hot water.

If you have no view from
your bath, create something
to look at while you
unwind, like this beautiful
mural of spring blossom on
the wall. A single, candy-
pink long-stemmed rose
with a delicate perfume is
in a vintage pitcher nearby.

To create a calm space to unwind at the end of the day, but also go about your daily ablutions, you need clever storage for toiletries and towels. Here the owner has created hidden storage by building a second wall deeper into the room. Warm woods on the floor and the exterior bath panel create an elegant seamless look, and add a natural color to balance the burnt orange and cool taupe.

threesome with a contemporary wooden basin, a chic "floating" wall-hung toilet, and a rolltop bathtub with claw feet.

For showers, you can either opt for a wet room or a conventional shower. A wet area is simply a section of the room that has been made watertight, with tiles, rubber, or another waterproof material, where the floor slopes slightly so water flows out through a central pipe. These walk-in shower areas are indulgent, but they require careful planning as you don't want to get everything else wet, too, like your towel rod and toilet.

Storage is often an issue in bathrooms, so include somewhere to keep your lotions and potions. Contemporary bathroom cabinets (in all shapes and sizes) are often mirror-fronted and wall-hung, so they double as dressing mirrors. Old dressers look as at home in a modern bathroom as they do in the bedroom, while side

ABOVE LEFT **Bathrooms need a mix of lighting, from task lighting for makeup and shaving to ambient lighting to relax by. Here a duo of wall-mounted downlights is perfectly placed above twin mirrors for task lights, while a collection of candles on an elegant side table creates a gentle, soothing atmosphere.**

ABOVE RIGHT **Black slate tiles on the bath surround and walls make a bold statement against a white ceramic tub and ceiling.**

tables and nests of tables make perfect spots to display vintage perfume bottles and scented candles. You'll also want a place to stash bathroom linens. Store them somewhere they will get air and light, for example old bookcases, armoires, or big wicker baskets.

Accessorize with nature's bounty. Bathrooms are the one place in the home where we can relax completely, so make sure you have some beautiful flowers or potted plants in view. Last, when bathing, you can also indulge in nature. Sprinkle rose petals on your bathwater and add drops of calming essential oils.

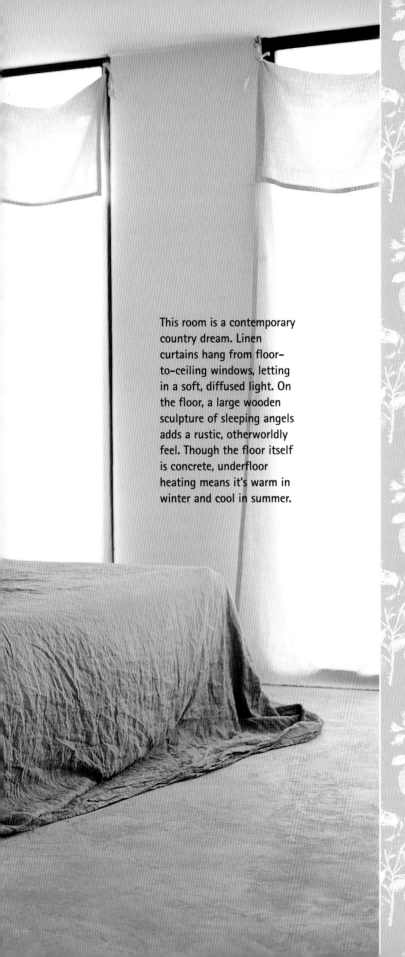

This room is a contemporary country dream. Linen curtains hang from floor-to-ceiling windows, letting in a soft, diffused light. On the floor, a large wooden sculpture of sleeping angels adds a rustic, otherworldly feel. Though the floor itself is concrete, underfloor heating means it's warm in winter and cool in summer.

sleeping

No other room so welcomes contemporary country as the bedroom. When decked out with all nature's materials—feathers, fabrics, linens, and fur—a bedroom soothes and placates the spirit, just what you need for a peaceful, restful sleep.

One of the things we love about escaping to a rustic idyll is the quality of our sleep, away from light pollution and inner-city din. Even in urban spaces you can recreate a sense of tranquility by making sure bedrooms are tucked away from street sounds and having your windows double-glazed. Soundproofing—putting insulation in ceilings and floors—will also quieten neighborly noise.

To keep out intruding light, cover your windows with blackout blinds. Alternatively, you could sew blackout fabric to the back of your curtains, and the extra layering will also provide another layer of sound insulation. Other ways to keep out light include a traditional country solution: shutters. In the French countryside, the shutters are so thick that not one little chink of light comes in—and they also prevent heat from escaping in winter.

In the morning, natural light helps wake us out of our slumber. When you draw your curtains, you'll want to let in the light but retain your privacy, so cover the lower half of the windows with an opaque covering such as voile, loose-weave linen, a vintage lace curtain, or even a decorative piece of wallpaper. Other options include sandblasted glass or a shade that rolls up from the bottom, in an opaque or punctured fabric. For flexible privacy, you could also use a fold-out screen.

When choosing a color scheme, pick a shade that soothes you. Calming colors that require next to no effort to live with include off-whites, neutrals, lavenders, pale blues, and soft peaches. These colors also marry well with the

> For a fresh chic country feel, expose your bed frame if it is made from natural materials. Show off its thick wooden legs or rusting iron structure.

muted hues of natural materials such as organic white linens, creamy sheepskins, and blond or walnut-colored wood.

Choose a floor covering that is kind to feet, like soft carpet. If you have wooden floors, put a sheepskin or goatskin beside your bed, so your feet don't meet a cold hard surface first thing in the morning.

To create a soft nest to slumber in, start with the bedroom's centerpiece, the bed. Many types of bed suit the look. Once again, mix country and modern versions for maximum comfort and aesthetic appeal. Traditional bed styles, like a sleigh or wooden bateau-lit bed, are easily brought up to date with geometric-patterned cushions on top of fresh, white linens, while contemporary versions such

ABOVE LEFT AND RIGHT **Tucked away in the quiet attic of a country home, this bedroom also has a sitting area. Soft furnishings give the room a relaxed feel: a rattan mat cloaks the floor, while fresh cottons dress a contemporary four-poster bed, the room's focal point.**

OPPOSITE **With a churchlike window, this attic bedroom feels like a sanctuary. The exposed beams and dyed sheepskins give it a country twist, while a modern floor lamp with a burnt-red shade and silk cushions on the bed give it an equally contemporary look.**

as a modern four-poster or a low-level futon can easily be countrified with patchwork and crocheted blankets. Otherwise, for a fresh chic country feel, expose your bed frame if it is made from natural materials. Show off its thick wooden legs or slightly rusting iron structure. If the frame is covered, you can accessorize your headboard with natural fabrics like suede, leather, silk, or linen.

If the frame is the bed's backbone, the mattress is its flesh. Natural fibers breathe more easily than manmade, so look for a mattress stuffed with soft yet firm fibers like cotton, coconut hair, or horsehair. A pocket-sprung mattress, or one sprung with individual metal coils, gives your spine the best support and prevents partner roll.

For comfort, you'll need to slumber in sheets that breathe with you, meaning natural materials like linen, cotton, or silk. Linen sheets don't wear out for decades, so although the cost may seem breathtaking, consider how much wear you will get out of them. Cotton sheets are easy to come by, but only buy those made from good-quality cotton, or they will become threadbare in no time. Treat your skin to glossy, luxurious silk sheets. Silk is often worn by athletes because it is light and breathable but warm— the perfect cover for summer when temperatures drop in the middle of the night, but rise quickly in early morning.

Duvets are the perfect no-fuss option for keeping warm. They come in a number of weighting and filling options. Goose down or fine duck down is the most luxurious choice; make sure the filling is

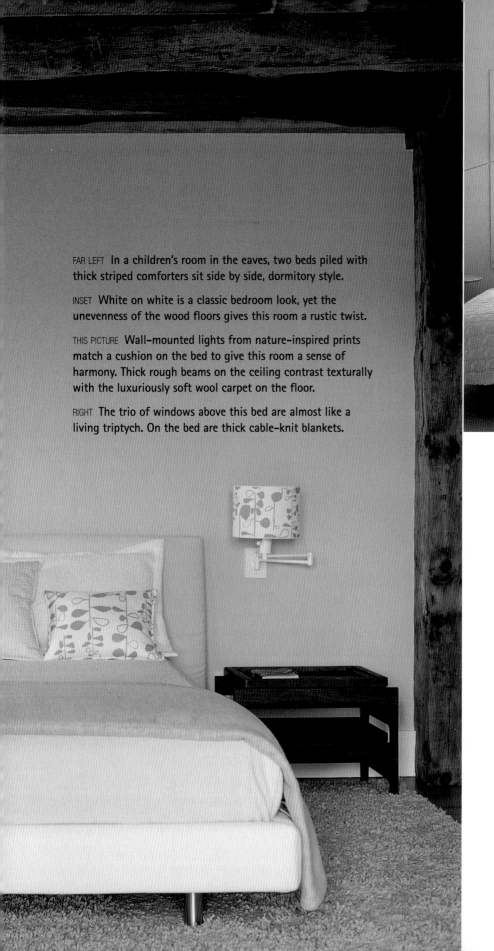

FAR LEFT In a children's room in the eaves, two beds piled with thick striped comforters sit side by side, dormitory style.

INSET White on white is a classic bedroom look, yet the unevenness of the wood floors gives this room a rustic twist.

THIS PICTURE Wall-mounted lights from nature-inspired prints match a cushion on the bed to give this room a sense of harmony. Thick rough beams on the ceiling contrast texturally with the luxuriously soft wool carpet on the floor.

RIGHT The trio of windows above this bed are almost like a living triptych. On the bed are thick cable-knit blankets.

stitched into individual compartments to prevent feathers from gathering at your feet. If you can't find a duvet cover to match the look, try making your own by sewing two antique linen sheets together and dyeing them to suit your room.

Some of us prefer the versatility of blankets, which can be piled on in the winter or peeled off in summer. Look for blankets made from cashmere, mohair, or other pure wools, as they are warm and let air circulate through their fibers. Antique and secondhand markets brim with blankets, including tartan and plaid, crocheted throws, and more. If nothing suitable turns up, consider buying a selection of small blankets of equal weight and sewing them together to make a country-style patchwork.

Patchwork quilts have always been a mainstay of the country style, yet they

don't need to look old-fashioned. Once crafted by economical housewives, with their intricate designs and beautiful stitching they have come to be regarded as pieces of art in their own right. Create your own contemporary version from vintage silk scarves, funky Fifties' designs, and retro clothing.

Your duvet, sheets, and blankets make a neutral canvas for nature's textiles. Create cushions from old silk or lace scarves and vintage paisley or floral fabrics and change them to suit the seasons. Adorn the end of your bed with a quiet contrast, like pieces of lace or embroidered tablecloths, fabric bolt ends, vintage curtains sewn together, silk saris, animal skins, or a pashmina shawl.

Soft shades of pink, oyster, fresh white, blossom, and magnolia blend together to create a calm, safe haven for sleep. The owner has kept the look startlingly plain, but what is in the room is simply beautiful. The crisp white bed linens and small white side table are basics; however, the nature-inspired canvas and the antique candelabra add a touch of feminine sophistication.

The bedroom is on a mezzanine, which allows light from the side windows to light the entire space. Surrounded by white walls, the sleeping area looks as if it is almost floating. Draped over the rail, pieces of luxurious fabrics and clothing add a sense of glamour to the interior.

versions in natural finishes, making sure that they suit the look.

Although you want to keep furnishings simple, you'll need a small bedside table for a reading light, books, water glass, and so on. You'll find plenty of occasional tables, wooden side tables, or even old school desks that fit in with the look. Or opt for something ultra-modern, like a clear plastic or molded-glass table.

Always have something beautiful beside your bed, such as fresh flowers or a scented candle, to help set your mood to "happy" for the day. Choose fragrant blooms—lavender, tuberoses, tiger lilies, freesias—and your nose will thank you, too. Wherever possible, let fresh air waft in throughout the night or morning to help keep your head clear.

> Adorn the end of your bed with a quiet contrast, like pieces of lace or embroidered tablecloths, vintage curtains sewn together, or a pashmina shawl.

For visual peace, this is one room in the home that should be clutterfree. For most of us the bedroom doubles as a dressing room, so adequate storage is essential. To keep lines pared down, hide your things by building in a wall of storage (see page 31) to house your entire wardrobe, either with push-catches or clear-glass handles. Sort out-of-season clothes into antique suitcases and wicker baskets, which you can tuck beneath your bed. Otherwise, choose elegant antique wood armoires and chests of drawers, or contemporary

ABOVE **A gray felt headboard highlights the dark wood bed frame and provides a somber visual contrast to colorful Welsh blankets at the foot of this bed. Where you can, wake up to nature's beautiful ornaments, like the duo of flowers here.**

RIGHT **One of the most alluring features of this peaceful bedroom is the presence of a handsome stove. This bed is brought to life with an antique country quilt.**

A garden gnome table, by French design maestro Philippe Starck, brings outdoor humor indoors. This calm attic room is given visual vibrancy with clashing geometric bed linen. On the wooden floor, a pug takes a dognap on a welcoming animal skin.

The wonderful thing about a contemporary country work area is that it doesn't have to look like an office at all. Place your desk near a window to bring nature in, seen here in butterfly pictures on the walls, a topiary potted plant, and a woven wire wastebasket.

working

We all need somewhere at home to pay bills, surf the internet, and write letters, even if it's a simple desk and a chair. Office spaces in the home are increasingly important as work becomes more flexible (or demanding), meaning we can work away from the office. Some of us run small businesses from home, too.

Yet home offices needn't be officelike. With a contemporary country twist, we can make the experience of sitting at a desk comfortable, functional, and rewarding. To begin, ditch the stereotypical office look. Contemporary country is miles away from low-ceilinged partitions, air-conditioning, stuffy desks and chairs, and fluorescent strip lights. Instead, create a sunlight-filled, airy space brimming with nature's accessories.

To find a place to work, create your own niche, perhaps in an alcove or corner if you don't have a whole room to spare. If possible, find a spot for your work station under large windows, where you can refresh your mind with a natural view (and the fresh air will keep you alert).

Next, you'll need a desk—the bigger the better, so you have plenty of room to spread out. You could use an old school desk or dining-room table, or mount a big piece of wood on a pair of trestles, which you can customize with a fresh coat of paint or cover with a linen cloth. If you're space-pressed, a glass desktop on metal supports will keep your room looking airy and light (glass can be cold to lean on, so wooden desks are a more tactile choice).

The chair at which you sit to work is very important for keeping your posture correctly aligned. You'll need one that keeps you bolt upright, with your feet firmly planted on the floor and your arms at right angles to the desk. Old office

BELOW This kitchen table is flanked by modern classic chairs from furnituremakers Charles and Ray Eames. The curvaceous chairs are placed in front of a large window so the owner can look out at a natural view as a break from the computer screen.

LEFT It's good to exercise your eye muscles. A lot of home work involves using screens and keyboards, so it's important to look out from time to time at distant horizons. A wicker basket houses all the desk's odds and ends.

OPPOSITE A tongue-and-groove wall, ceiling, and wooden floor in fresh white, mid-browns, and black provide a canvas for this utilitarian desk, chair, and adjustable light. Candle wall sconces and a silver candelabra bejeweled with bright blue candles soften the working atmosphere. Odds and ends are stored in dainty Arab-style brass tea glasses on a brass tray.

Juxtapose hi-tech equipment with naturally inspired desk accessories. Keep necessities in country-style tins, wicker baskets, teacups, vases and milk jugs.

chairs are obviously suited to the job, but make sure they look like they're on vacation, not at work, by reupholstering the seats in funky fabrics. For a rustic look, you could opt for old café seats, school chairs, or dining chairs.

A sturdy gooseneck light will prevent eyestrain and cast a suitably strong light on your work. You could customize an office-style lamp with a shell necklace or garland of fake flowers. Even though this is a work space, ambient lighting like candlelight will turn it into a place to daydream, too. Juxtapose hi-tech equipment such as computers and printers with naturally inspired desk accessories. For example, keep pens, paperclips, and other necessities in country-style tins, wicker baskets, teacups, glass vases, and milk jugs. Put larger paper files in old armoires, hutches, and industrial-style filing cabinets. To inspire you, keep reminders of the important things in life in view. Adorn your desk with fresh flowers, pebbles, family photos, or whatever brings you fond memories.

sources

...great for contemporary country decorative pieces ...

ALTAMIRA LIGHTING
79 Joyce Street
Warren, RI 02885
(401) 245-7676
www.altamiralighting.com
Contemporary table and floor lamps.

ANTHROPOLOGIE
1801 Walnut Street
Philadelphia, PA 19103
(215) 568-2114
Call (800) 309-2500 to find a store near you or visit the website.
www.anthropologie.com
Vintage-inspired one-of-a-kind home accessories, including decorative hooks, boxes, cupboard knobs, and racks.

THE CONTAINER STORE
725 Lexington Avenue
New York, NY 10022
(212) 366-4200
Call (888) 266-8246 or visit the website for a retail outlet near you.
www.thecontainerstore.com
An organizer's dream, this store is filled with containers and storage systems.

FISHS EDDY
889 Broadway
New York, NY 10003
(212) 420-9020
www.fishseddy.com
Overstock supplies of simple china mugs, plates, and bowls.

HABLE CONSTRUCTION
117 Perry Street
New York, NY 10014
(877) HABLE-04
www.hableconstruction.com
The New York shop is a furnisher's haven. The online catalog has a good range of nature-inspired contemporary printed fabric homewares.

HOLD EVERYTHING
Call (888) 922-4117 or visit the website for a store near you.
www.holdeverything.com
Everything for storage, from baskets to racks to bins to shelves.

KNOLL
1235 Water Street
East Greenville, PA 18041
(800) 343-5665
www.knoll.com
Selection of modern and ergonomic lamps.

PALECEK
The Design Pavilion #27
200 Kansas Street
San Francisco, CA 94103
(800) 274-7730
www.palecek.com
Painted wicker furniture and accessories with an exotic feel.

PIER ONE IMPORTS
71 Fifth Avenue
New York, NY 10003
(212) 206-1911
Visit the website to find a store near you.
www.pier1.com
Decorative home accessories, often in wicker or rattan, organize your home to a world beat.

R 20TH CENTURY DESIGN
82 Franklin Street
New York, NY 10013
(212) 343-7979
www.r20thcentury.com
Includes a comprehensive selection of mid-century modern lamps and lighting fixtures.

STONE PANELS
100 South Royal Lane
Coppell, TX 75019
(800) 328-6275
www.stonepanels.com
Stone surfaces, from limestone to granite to marble, for walls.

THE TIN BIN
20 Valley Road
Neffsville, PA 17601
(717) 569-6210
www.thetinbin.com
Wide choice of lamps for indoor and outdoor use.

URBAN OUTFITTERS
628 Broadway
New York, NY 10012
(212) 475-0009
Visit the website to find the retail outlet near you.
www.urbanoutfitters.com
Trendy and affordable home accessories include an ever-changing selection of retro storage boxes, baskets, and wall hooks.

VINTAGE BASKETS
20212 Eighty-seventh Avenue South
Kent, WA 98031
(253) 395-3131
A wide selection of baskets offer both storage and style.

WILLIAMSBURG MARKETPLACE CATALOG
(800) 414-6291
www.williamsburgmarketplace.com
Historically accurate reproductions of Colonial pewter, prints, and other decorative accessories.

...great for contemporary country classic and modern pieces...

ABC CARPET & HOME
888 Broadway
New York, NY 10003
(212) 473-3000
www.abchome.com
An eclectic collection of antique and contemporary furnishings, including wardrobes, sideboards, chests of drawers, and end tables.

THE CONRAN SHOP
Bridgemarket
407 East 59th Street
New York, NY 10022
(212) 755-9079
www.conran.com
Beautifully designed modern furniture for every room, plus a good selection of storage boxes and baskets.

COUNTRY FRENCH INTERIORS
1428 Slocum Street
Dallas, TX 75207
(214) 747-4700
www.countryfrenchinteriors.com
18th- and 19th-century French antiques.

CRATE & BARREL
646 North Michigan Avenue
Chicago, IL 60611
(800) 967-6696
www.crateandbarrel.com
A great source of good-value furniture and storage accessories.

ETHAN ALLEN
Ethan Allen Drive
Danbury, CT 06813
(203) 743-8500
Visit the website for an outlet near you.
www.ethanallen.com
Reproduction antiques for every room, from dining to bedroom to home office.

FIREPLACE EQUIPMENT WAREHOUSE
1002 North Central Expressway
Richardson, TX 75080
(972) 783-6988
www.fireplaceequipment.com
Wood-burning and gas fireplaces and fireplace surrounds.

GEORGE SMITH
142 North Robertson Boulevard
Los Angeles, CA 90048
(310) 360-0880
www.georgesmith.com
English sofas and chairs.

GRACIOUS HOME
1220 Third Avenue
New York, NY 10021
(212) 517-6300
www.gracioushome.com
Fine vanities, shelves, trolleys, and cabinets.

HERMAN MILLER INC.
855 East Main Avenue
P.O. Box 302
Zeeland, MI 49464
(800) 646-4400
www.hermanmiller.com
Official U.S. importer of Artek furniture, including Alvar Aalto and other fine 20th-century furniture designers.

LAURA ASHLEY HOME STORE
171 East Ridgewood Avenue
Ridgewood, NJ 07450
(201) 670-0688
www.lauraashley-usa.com
Tasteful selection of reproduction cabinets, armoires, sideboards, dressing tables, and more, including glamorous Thirties-style mirrored furniture.

MAINE COTTAGE FURNITURE
106 Lafayette Street
Lower Falls Landing
Yarmouth, ME 04096
(888) 859-5522
www.mainecottage.com
Simple, hardworking furniture for every room of the house.

POTTERY BARN
600 Broadway
New York, NY 10012
(212) 219-2420
Visit the website for an outlet near you.
www.potterybarn.com
Pieces for every room.

RESTORATION HARDWARE
935 Broadway
New York, NY 10010
(212) 260-9479
Visit the website for an outlet near you.
www.restorationhardware.com
Practical but handsome furniture and hardware.

SHAKER STYLE
292 Chesham Road
Harrisville, NH 03450
(888) 824-3340
www.shakerstyle.com
Custom-built Shaker-style furniture.

STONE MAGIC
301 Pleasant Drive
Dallas, TX 75217
(800) 597-3606
www.stonemagic.com
Cast-stone fireplaces and mantels.

WILKENING FIREPLACE
9608 State 371 NW
Walker, MN 56484
Call (800) 367-7976 for a retailer
near you.
www.wilkeningfireplace.com
*Fireplaces, wood stoves, screens,
and enclosures.*

...great for underfoot...

AGED WOODS INC.
2331 East Market Street
York, PA 17402
(800) 233-9307
www.agedwoods.com
*Antique heart pine, hickory, ash, and
other unusual flooring.*

PARIS CERAMICS
150 East 58th Street, 7th Floor
New York, NY 10155
(212) 644-2782
www.parisceramics.com
*Limestone, terracotta, antique stone,
and hand-painted tiles.*

**...great for contemporary country
textiles, wallpapers, and paint...**

CALICO CORNERS
1610 Cochran Road
Pittsburgh, PA 15220
(412) 344-4840
Call (800) 213-6366 for other locations.
www.calicocorners.com
*Designer fabrics. Stores nationwide and
by mail order.*

CLARENCE HOUSE FABRICS, LTD.
979 Third Avenue, Suite 205
New York, NY 10022
(800) 221-4704
www.clarencehouse.com
*Natural-fiber fabrics with prints based
on 15th- to 20th-century patterns. Also
hand-woven textiles and fine wallpapers.*

GARNET HILL
231 Main Street
Franconia, NH 03580
(800) 870-3513
www.garnethill.com
*Bed linen in natural fibers; down
comforters and pillows.*

HANCOCK FABRICS
2605A West Main Street
Tupelo, MS 38801
(662) 844-7368
Call (877) 322-7427 for branches.
www.hancockfabrics.com
America's largest fabric store.

PIERRE DEUX
625 Madison Avenue
New York, NY 10022
(212) 521-8012
www.pierredeux.com
*French country fabric, upholstery,
wallpaper, and antiques.*

SALAMANDRE SILK, INC.
950 Third Avenue
New York, NY 10022
(718) 361-8500
*Restores classic fabrics and sells
adaptations for home use, as well
as trims and notions. Houses the
Museum of Textiles.*

**...great for second-hand and
salvage...**

BRIMFIELD ANTIQUE SHOW
Route 20
Brimfield, MA 01010
www.brimfieldshow.com
*This famous flea market, which features
dealers from all over the U.S. and from
Europe, runs for a week in May, July, and
September. For listings of other flea
markets around the country, visit
www.fleamarket.com.*

UP THE CREEK ANTIQUES
209 North Tower
Centralia, WA 98531
(800) 246-0868
www.amerantfurn.com
*American furniture and lighting in
Victorian, Eastlake, turn-of-the-century,
Mission, Arts and Crafts, Depression, and
1940s Classic Revival periods, in both
restored and original finish.*

**...great for contemporary country
cooking and eating spaces...**

AGA RANGES
110 Woodcrest Road
Cherry Hill, NJ 08003
(800) 633-9200
www.aga-ranges.com
*Cast-iron cooking and heating appliances,
and own branded cookware range.*

ANTIQUE HARDWARE & HOME
(800) 422-9982
www.antiquehardware.com
*Unusual and antique hardware
and fixtures.*

HARRINGTON BRASSWORKS
(201) 818-1300
www.harringtonbrassworks.com
*Brass fixtures for kitchen and home,
especially faucets. Also bathroom
products.*

POGGENPOHL
350 Passaic Avenue
Fairfield, NJ 07004
(973) 812-8900
www.poggenpohl-usa.com
Customized kitchen design.

VIKING
111 Front Street
Greenwood, MS 38930
(888) 845-4641
www.vikingrange.com
*Professional-style cookers and
refrigerators.*

WILLIAMS-SONOMA
121 East 59th Street
New York, NY 10022
(917) 369-1131
(877) 812-6235 for information
www.williams-sonoma.com
*Cooking utensils, fine linens, and
classic china.*

**....great for contemporary
country bathing...**

BED, BATH & BEYOND
620 Avenue of the Americas
New York, NY 10011
(212) 255-3550
Visit the website for a store near you.
www.bedbathandbeyond.com.
*Everything for the bathroom, including
storage solutions in a variety of styles
and prices.*

KALLISTA
444 Highland Drive
Mailstop 032
Kohler, WI 53044
(888) 4-KALLISTA
www.kallistainc.com
Luxury bathroom hardware and details.

PORTICO BED & BATH
72 Spring Street
New York, NY 10012
(212) 941-7800
(877) 517-8800 for mail order
www.porticostore.com
White linens, towels, and bath accessories.

TAKAGI INDUSTRIAL CO. USA, INC.
(888) 882-5244
www.takagi-usa.com
Special large, deep Japanese bathtubs.

VINTAGE PLUMBING
9645 Sylvia Avenue
Northridge, CA 91324
(818) 772-1721
www.vintageplumbing.com
*Original and restored to perfection
bathroom antiques, including pull-
chain toilets and clawfoot bathtubs.*

WATERWORKS
23 West Putnam Avenue
Greenwich, CT 06830
(203) 869-7766
www.waterworks.com
*Smart selection of modern bathroom
storage and accessories.*

WONDER SHOWER
(800) 595-0385
www.showeringgifts.com
*Shower heads made from brushed nickel,
brass, copper, platinum, and chrome in
sloping, extension, or dual arm designs.*

...useful...

ANDERSEN WINDOWS AND DOORS
100 Fourth Avenue North
Bayport, MN 55003
(800) 426-4261
www.andersenwindows.com
*All types of windows and doors, including
patio doors. Also traditional-style window
and door furniture.*

**THE ASSOCIATED GENERAL
CONTRACTORS OF AMERICA**
2300 Wilson Boulevard, Suite 400
Arlington, VA 22201
(703) 548-3118
www.AGC.org
*Trade organization that will help you
locate contractors.*

**CHIMNEY SAFETY INSTITUTE
OF AMERICA**
2155 Commercial Drive
Plainfield, IN 46168
(317) 837-5362
www.csia.org
*Public safety and information
organization.*

FEDERAL TRADE COMMISSION (FTC)
Consumer Response Center
600 Pennsylvania Avenue, NW
Washington, D.C. 20580
www.FTC.gov
*Refers consumers to appropriate agency
for remodeling contractors and offers
advice about how to work with them.*

VELUX AMERICA INC.
450 Old Brickyard Road
Greenwood, SC 29648
(800) 888-3589
www.velux-america.com
Roof windows and skylights.

picture credits

All photographs by Debi Treloar.

KEY: **a**=above, **b**=below, **r**=right, **l**=left, **c**=center.

Endpapers Jacqueline Morabito's home in La Colle-Sur-Loup, France; **1** Bernt Heiberg of Heiberg Cummings Design's home in the Hamptons, New York; **2–3** Vine Cottage (and "Moogi" the dog); **4–5** Sanne Hjermind and Claes Bech-Poulsen; **6** Marcus Hewitt and Susan Hopper's home in Litchfield County, Connecticut; **7** Christina and Allan Thaulow's home in Denmark; **8–9** Carolyn Quatermaine's home in La Colle-Sur-Loup, South of France; **10** Josephine Macrander, Interior Decorator; **11a** Marcus Hewitt and Susan Hopper's home in Litchfield County, Connecticut; **11b** Sanne Hjermind and Claes Bech-Poulsen; **12–13** Ceramicist Jette Arendal Winther's home in Denmark, www.arendal-ceramics.com; **14–15** Rupert Spira's house in Shropshire; **16a** Bernt Heiberg of Heiberg Cummings Design's home in the Hamptons, New York; **16b** Ceramicist Jette Arendal Winther's home in Denmark, www.arendal-ceramics.com; **17al & c** Sanne Hjermind and Claes Bech-Poulsen; **17ar** Jacqueline Morabito's home in La Colle-Sur-Loup, France; **17b** Carolyn Quatermaine's home in La Colle-Sur-Loup, South of France; **18** Sanne Hjermind and Claes Bech-Poulsen; **19** Michael Leva's home in Litchfield County, Connecticut; **20** Ceramicist Jette Arendal Winther's home in Denmark, www.arendal-ceramics.com; **21** Michael Leva's home in Litchfield County, Connecticut; **22–23** Bernt Heiberg of Heiberg Cummings Design's home in the Hamptons, New York; **24al** Marcus Hewitt and Susan Hopper's home in Litchfield County, Connecticut; **24ar** Michael Leva's home in Litchfield County, Connecticut; **24b** Available for photographic location at www.inspacelocations.com; **25** Marcus Hewitt and Susan Hopper's home in Litchfield County, Connecticut; **26** A country house rebuilt and extended by James Gorst Architects; **27l** Private residence in Washington, Connecticut; **27r** Rupert Spira's house in Shropshire; **28** Marcus Hewitt and Susan Hopper's home in Litchfield County, Connecticut; **29** Private residence in Washington, Connecticut; **30al** Vine Cottage; **30ar & b** Michael Leva's home in Litchfield County, Connecticut; **31** Bernt Heiberg of Heiberg Cummings Design's home in the Hamptons, New York; **32** Vine Cottage; **33** Private residence in Washington, Connecticut; **34** Available for photographic location at www.inspacelocations.com; **35al & br** Vine Cottage; **35ar** Catherine Samy and Richard Lewis's Suffolk house designed by Geoff Pyle and Ben Kilburn; **35bl** Rupert Spira's house in Shropshire; **35c** Josephine Macrander, Interior Decorator; **36al** Sanne Hjermind and Claes Bech-Poulsen; **36ac** Bernt Heiberg of Heiberg Cummings Design's home in the Hamptons, New York; **36r** Josephine Macrander, Interior Decorator; **36bl** Ceramicist Jette Arendal Winther's home in Denmark, www.arendal-ceramics.com; **37** Christina and Allan Thaulow's home in Denmark; **38** Ceramicist Jette Arendal Winther's home in Denmark, www.arendal-ceramics.com; **39al & b** Sanne Hjermind and Claes Bech-Poulsen; **39ar** Ceramicist Jette Arendal Winther's home in Denmark, www.arendal-ceramics.com; **40–41** Bernt Heiberg of Heiberg Cummings Design's home in the Hamptons, New York; **42–43** Rupert Spira's house in Shropshire; **43c** Vine Cottage; **43r** Josephine Macrander, Interior Decorator; **44l** Private residence in Washington, Connecticut; **44c** Marcus Hewitt and Susan Hopper's home in Litchfield County, Connecticut; **44r** Michael Leva's home in Litchfield County, Connecticut; **45** A country house rebuilt and extended by James Gorst Architects; **46a & 47** Jacqueline Morabito's home in La Colle-Sur-Loup, France; **46bl** Catherine Samy and Richard Lewis's Suffolk house designed by Geoff Pyle and Ben Kilburn; **46br** Roeline Faber, Interior Designer; **48 & 49a** Ceramicist Jette Arendal Winther's home in Denmark, www.arendal-ceramics.com; **49b** Wim Kloosterboer, Made Architecten, Rotterdam, The Netherlands; **50–51** Christina and Allan Thaulow's home in Denmark; **52 & 53r** Private residence in Washington, Connecticut; **53l** A country house rebuilt and extended by James Gorst Architects; **54** Wim Kloosterboer, Made Architecten, Rotterdam, The Netherlands; **55al** Christina and Allan Thaulow's home in Denmark; **55ar & b** Sanne Hjermind and Claes Bech-Poulsen; **56al & c** A country house rebuilt and extended by James Gorst Architects; **56ar** Ceramicist Jette Arendal Winther's home in Denmark, www.arendal-ceramics.com; **56b** Private residence in Washington, Connecticut; **57al** Josephine Macrander, Interior Decorator; **57ar** Christina and Allan Thaulow's home in Denmark; **57bl** Catherine Samy and Richard Lewis's Suffolk house designed by Geoff Pyle and Ben Kilburn; **58l** Bernt Heiberg of Heiberg Cummings Design's home in the Hamptons, New York; **58–60** Jacqueline Morabito's home in La Colle-Sur-Loup, France; **59 inset** Ceramicist Jette Arendal Winther's home in Denmark, www.arendal-ceramics.com; **61al** A country house rebuilt and extended by James Gorst Architects; **61ac** Rupert Spira's house in Shropshire; **61ar** Carolyn Quatermaine's home in La Colle-Sur-Loup, South of France; **61b** Catherine Samy and Richard Lewis's Suffolk house designed by Geoff Pyle and Ben Kilburn; **62–3** Rupert Spira's house in Shropshire; **62 inset** Carolyn Quatermaine's home in La Colle-Sur-Loup, South of France; **63r** Available for photographic location at www.inspace locations.com; **64l** Vine Cottage; **64ar** Ceramicist Jette Arendal Winther's home in Denmark, www.arendal-ceramics.com; **64br** Josephine Macrander, Interior Decorator; **65** Catherine Samy and Richard Lewis's Suffolk house designed by Geoff Pyle and Ben Kilburn; **66–7** Jacqueline Morabito's home in La Colle-Sur-Loup, France; **66 inset** Private residence in Washington, Connecticut; **68–71** Available for photographic location at www.inspacelocations.com; **70b** Catherine Samy and Richard Lewis's Suffolk house designed by Geoff Pyle and Ben Kilburn; **72** Bernt Heiberg of Heiberg Cummings Design's home in the Hamptons, New York; **73** Josephine Macrander, Interior Decorator; **74–75** Roeline Faber, Interior Designer; **76a** Rupert Spira's house in Shropshire; **76b** Sanne Hjermind and Claes Bech-Poulsen; **77** Jacqueline Morabito's home in La Colle-Sur-Loup, France; **78–79** Josephine Macrander, Interior Decorator; **78 inset** Rupert Spira's house in Shropshire; **79r** Available for photographic location at www.inspace locations.com; **80–81** Jacqueline Morabito's home in La Colle-Sur-Loup, France; **82–83** Roeline Faber, Interior Designer; **84l** A country house rebuilt and extended by James Gorst Architects; **84r** Marcus Hewitt and Susan Hopper's home in Litchfield County, Connecticut; **85** Private residence in Washington, Connecticut; **86l** Sanne Hjermind and Claes Bech-Poulsen; **86–7** Vine Cottage; **87r** Michael Leva's home in Litchfield County, Connecticut; **88–89** Josephine Macrander, Interior Decorator; **90–91 & 91b** Available for photographic location at www.inspacelocations.com; **91a** Josephine Macrander, Interior Decorator; **92l** Sanne Hjermind and Claes Bech-Poulsen; **92r–93** Christina and Allan Thaulow's home in Denmark; **94–95** Marcus Hewitt and Susan Hopper's home in Litchfield County, Connecticut; **95r** Catherine Samy and Richard Lewis's Suffolk house designed by Geoff Pyle and Ben Kilburn; **96–97** Carolyn Quatermaine's home in La Colle-Sur-Loup, South of France; **98l** Rupert Spira's house in Shropshire; **98–99** Ceramicist Jette Arendal Winther's home in Denmark, www.arendal-ceramics.com; **100–101** Michael Leva's home in Litchfield County, Connecticut; **102–103** Bernt Heiberg of Heiberg Cummings Design's home in the Hamptons, New York; **103r** Roeline Faber, Interior Designer; **104–105** Wim Kloosterboer, Made Architecten, Rotterdam, The Netherlands; **106–107** Christina and Allan Thaulow's home in Denmark; **108–109** Catherine Samy and Richard Lewis's Suffolk house designed by Geoff Pyle and Ben Kilburn; **110** Marcus Hewitt and Susan Hopper's home in Litchfield County, Connecticut; **111** Private residence in Washington, Connecticut; **112–113** A country house rebuilt and extended by James Gorst Architects; **114–115** Jacqueline Morabito's home in La Colle-Sur-Loup, France; **116** Catherine Samy and Richard Lewis's Suffolk house designed by Geoff Pyle and Ben Kilburn; **117a** Private residence in Washington, Connecticut; **117b** Wim Kloosterboer, Made Architecten, Rotterdam, The Netherlands; **118l** Marcus Hewitt and Susan Hopper's home in Litchfield County, Connecticut; **118r** Private residence in Washington, Connecticut; **119** Vine Cottage; **120** Bernt Heiberg of Heiberg Cummings Design's home in the Hamptons, New York; **120 inset** Jacqueline Morabito's home in La Colle-Sur-Loup, France; **121** Carolyn Quatermaine's home in La Colle-Sur-Loup, South of France; **122** Catherine Samy and Richard Lewis's Suffolk house designed by Geoff Pyle and Ben Kilburn; **123l** Sanne Hjermind and Claes Bech-Poulsen; **123r** Michael Leva's home in Litchfield County, Connecticut; **124–125** Jacqueline Morabito's home in La Colle-Sur-Loup, France; **126** Michael Leva's home in Litchfield County, Connecticut; **127** Available for photographic location at www.inspacelocations.com; **128–129** Private residence in Washington, Connecticut; **128 inset** Michael Leva's home in Litchfield County, Connecticut; **130–131** Carolyn Quatermaine's home in La Colle-Sur-Loup, South of France; **132a** Vine Cottage; **132b** Catherine Samy and Richard Lewis's Suffolk house designed by Geoff Pyle and Ben Kilburn; **133** Marcus Hewitt and Susan Hopper's home in Litchfield County, Connecticut; **134–135** Michael Leva's home in Litchfield County, Connecticut; **135r** Marcus Hewitt and Susan Hopper's home in Litchfield County, Connecticut; **136** Sanne Hjermind and Claes Bech-Poulsen; **137** Roeline Faber, Interior Designer.

business credits

Artist Sanne Hjermind

T: +45 26 91 01 97

and Photographer Claes Bech-Poulsen

T: +45 40 19 93 99

claes@claesbp.com
www.claesbp.dk

Pages 4–5; 11b; 17al & c; 18; 36al; 39al & b; 55ar & b; 76b; 86b; 92l; 123l; 136.

Ben Kilburn

Cullum and Nightingale
Architects
61 Judd Street
London WC1H 9QT
T: +44 20 7383 4466

www.cullumnightingale.com

Pages 35ar; 46bl; 57bl; 61b; 65; 70b; 95r; 108–109; 116; 122; 132b.

Carolyn Quatermaine Studio

T: +44 20 7373 4492

www.carolynquatermaine.com

Pages 8–9; 17b; 61ar; 62 inset; 96–97; 121; 130–131.

Geoff Pyle

Pyle Associates
Bank Chambers
Cheapside
Langport
Somerset TA10 9PD
T: +44 1458 253050

www.pyleassociates.co.uk

Pages 35ar; 46bl; 57bl; 61b; 65; 70b; 95r; 108–109; 116; 122; 132b.

Heiberg Cummings Design

9 West 19th Street, 3rd Floor
New York, NY 10011
T: 212 337 2030
F: 212 337 2033

bheiberg@hcd3.com
wcummings@hcd3.com
www.hcd3.com

and

Heiberg Cummings Design

Gimleveien 22
0266 Oslo
Norway
T: +47 22 12 98 70
F: +47 22 12 98 79

eramm@hcd3.com

Pages 1; 16a; 22–23; 31; 36ac; 40–41; 58l; 72; 102–103; 120.

**Jacqueline Morabito/
JM Bureau de Style**

42–65 rue Yves Klein
06480 La Colle-Sur-Loup
France
T: +33 4 93 32 64 92
F: +33 4 93 32 54 94

jm@jacquelinemorabito.com

Endpapers; pages 17ar; 46a; 47; 58–60; 77; 80–81; 66–67; 114–115; 120 inset; 124–125.

James Gorst Architects

The House of Detention
Clerkenwell Close
London EC1R 0AS
T: +44 20 7336 7140

info@jamesgorstarchitects.com
www.jamesgorstarchitects.co.uk

Pages 26; 45; 53l; 56al & c; 61al; 84l; 112–113.

Jette Arendal Winther

www.arendal-ceramics.com

Pages 12–13; 16b; 20; 36bl; 38; 39ar; 48 & 49a; 56ar; 59 inset; 64ar; 98–99.

Josephine Macrander

Interior Decorator
T: +31 64 30 53 062

josephinemacrander@hetnet.nl

Pages 10; 35c; 36r; 43r; 57al; 64br; 73; 78–79; 88–89; 91a.

Made Architecten

Marconistraat 52
3029 AK Rotterdam
The Netherlands
T: +31 10 24 40 750
F: +31 10 24 40 752

www.madearchitecten.nl

Pages 49b; 54; 104–105; 117b.

Maisonette

79 Chamberlayne Road
London NW10 3ND
T: +44 20 8964 8444
F: +44 20 8964 8464

maisonetteuk@aol.com
www.maisonette.uk.com

Pages 24b; 34; 63r; 68–70a; 71; 79r; 90–91; 127.

Michael Leva

P.O. Box 100
Roxbury, CT 06783
T: 860 355 2225

Pages 19; 21; 24ar; 30ar & b; 44r; 87; 100–101; 123r; 126; 128 inset; 134–135.

Paul van der Kooi

(Kitchens)
Heliumweg 40A
3812 RE Amersfoort
The Netherlands
T: +31 33 46 51 111

www.heuhenopmaat.nl

Pages 46br; 82–3.

Roeline Faber Interior Styling & Design

Tweede Molenweg 22
1261 HC Blaricum
The Netherlands
T: +31 35 66 68 411

faber.styling@wxs.nl

Pages 46br; 74–75; 82–83; 103r; 137.

Rupert Spira

Church Farm
More
Bishop's Castle
Shropshire SY9 5HH
T: +44 1588 650588

Rupert@spira.ndo.co.uk
www.rupertspira.com

Pages 14–15; 27r; 35bl; 42–43; 61ac; 62–63; 76a; 78 inset; 98l.

Wim Kloosterboer

Made Architecten
Marconistraat 52
3029 AK Rotterdam
T: +31 10 24 40 750

mademail@xs4all.nl
www.madearchitecten.nl

Pages 49b; 54; 104–105; 117b.

index

NOTE: Page numbers in *italics* refer to captions.

acknowledgments

Emily Chalmers would like to thank everyone who made this book possible. Thanks to Alison Starling and Anne-Marie Bulat—the team behind the commission—and Clare Double and Paul Tilby who brought the book to life. Thanks also to Tracy Ogino, and all the contemporary country dwellers who gave us access to their wonderful homes.

Once again special thanks to Ali Hanan for taking the book a step further, and to Debi Treloar for all the wonderful images and her energy behind them.

About the Author

Roma Gans has called children "enlightened, excited citizens." She believes in the fundamental theory that children are eager to learn. Place the right teacher in the classroom with them, put good up-to-date books, magazines, and other materials in their reach, and children themselves whet their own intellectual curiosity.

Dr. Gans received her B.S. at Teachers College, Columbia University, and her M.A. and Ph.D. at Columbia University. She began her work in the educational field in the public schools of the Middle West as a teacher, supervisor, and then superintendent of schools. She is Professor Emeritus of Childhood Education at Teachers College, and lectures extensively throughout the United States and Canada. All of her research has been in the field of reading. Dr. Gans is the author of *Reading Is Fun, Guiding Children's Reading Through Experiences, Critical Reading in the Intermediate Grades*, and just recently, *Common Sense in Teaching Reading*. With Dr. Franklyn M. Branley, she is supervising and editing the Let's-Read-and-Find-Out books.

About the Illustrator

When he is not writing or illustrating, Ed Emberley pursues some interesting hobbies. He prints limited editions of children's books on his own hand press, studies Early Americana, and experiments with toy-making.

Mr. Emberley received a B.F.A. in illustration from the Massachusetts School of Art in Boston. He lives in Beverly, Massachusetts, with his wife and two young children.

You may eat three or four times a day,
Birds eat ten, thirty, and even fifty times a day.
They eat flies and gnats, bugs and caterpillars, worms
  and suet, seeds and berries.
Birds eat and eat and eat.
They seem to eat all day.

See how many birds will eat from your feeders.
They will come to your feeders every day.
Once they start coming you will be busy keeping
   your feeders filled.

Big and little woodpeckers will come to it.
They will eat and eat and eat.
Nuthatches, chickadees, and bluejays will eat the
    suet, too.

Birds eat and eat and eat.
You can see how much they eat.
Make a suet feeder.
Get some suet from a meat market.
Tie the suet to the branch of a tree.

The nuthatch pokes a sunflower seed into a small
   hole in the bark of a tree.
It pecks and pecks to open the seed.
It eats the kernel and flies to get another seed.

Birds eat in different ways.

The chickadee flies to a branch with a seed.

It holds the seed against the branch with its feet.

It pecks and pecks to open the shell.

It eats the kernel, then flies to the feeder to get another seed.

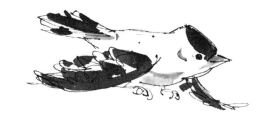

You can buy seeds for birds at the grocery store.

Once birds find your feeder they will eat and eat until it is empty.

Chickadees and goldfinches, blackbirds and nut-hatches may come.

They are seed eaters.

When your feeder is empty fill it again.

See how quickly the birds empty it.

Birds eat and eat and eat.

You can see how much they eat.

Make a feeder from an empty milk carton, the size
   that holds one glass of milk.

Cut off the cover.

The carton will be the feeder.

Punch holes on opposite sides near the top.

Put string through the holes to make a handle.

Hang the feeder from a shrub or low branch.

Fill it with seeds.

Birds eat and eat and eat.

You can see how much they eat.

Put some breadcrumbs on the ground near your
house.

Sparrows and bluejays and starlings will soon find
them.

See how quickly they eat the crumbs.

Woodpeckers get food from trees.
Have you ever watched a woodpecker go up and down
and around a tree?
It stops to rap on the tree with its beak.
It pecks holes in the tree to find the bugs and worms
under the bark.

Swallows and phoebes catch their food in the air as
    they fly.
They swoop and dive after gnats and insects.
As the phoebe catches an insect you can hear the
    bird click its beak.

Crows eat seeds, too.

They walk in a corn field and pull up plants that have
just started to grow.

They eat the seeds at the bottom of the plants.

A goldfinch sits on the sunflower and eats the seeds.
Chickadees perch on the branch of a shrub and eat
   the seeds.
They swing on the branch as they eat.

Fox sparrows and chewinks scratch and dig in the ground.
Robins pull worms right out of the ground.

Watch the birds to see how they eat.
Bluejays, sparrows, and juncos eat seeds off the ground.

It will eat hundreds of seeds and berries, too.

bugs and caterpillars, worms and insects.

Each day a bird may eat hundreds of flies and gnats,

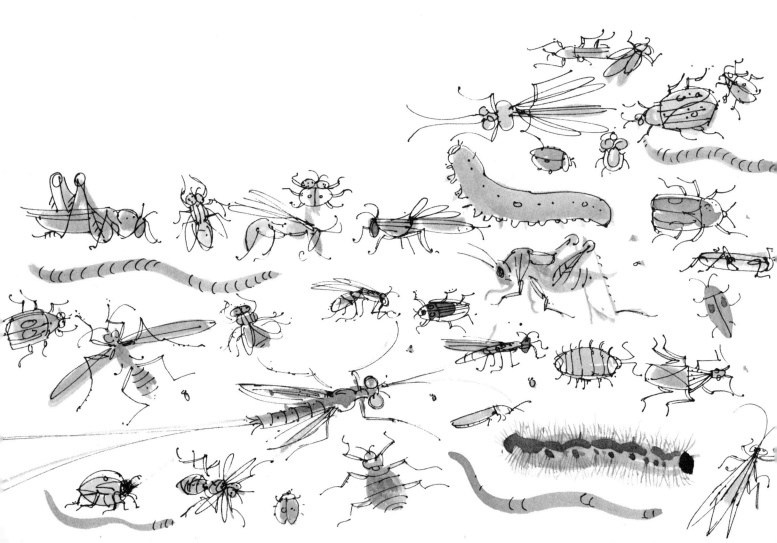

Birds eat and eat and eat.

They seem to eat all day.

How often do you eat?

    Three times a day?

    Four times a day?

    Five times a day?

Birds eat ten, thirty, and even fifty times a day.

Birds Eat and Eat and Eat

LET'S-READ-AND-FIND-OUT SCIENCE BOOKS

Editors: *DR. ROMA GANS*, Professor Emeritus of Childhood Education, Teachers College, Columbia University
DR. FRANKLYN M. BRANLEY, Chairman and Astronomer of The American Museum-Hayden Planetarium

*AVAILABLE IN SPANISH

ISBN: 0-690-14514-4
0-690-14515-2 (LB)

Published in Canada by Fitzhenry & Whiteside Limited, Toronto

4   5   6   7   8   9   10

and Eat and Eat

by Roma Gans | Illustrated by Ed Emberley

Birds Eat

Thomas Y. Crowell Company | New York

Birds Eat and Eat and Eat